Paul of Alexandria

Introduction to Astrology

Translated from the Greek
by
James Herschel Holden, M.A.
Fellow of the
American Federation
of Astrologers

ISBN-10: 0-86690-633-9
ISBN-13:978-0-86690-633-3

Editions 1 and 2 were not published, but were circulated privately as pho-
tocopies.

First printing of the third edition, 2012.

Cover Design: Jack Cipolla

Published by:
American Federation of Astrologers, Inc.
6535 S. Rural Road
Tempe, AZ 85283

www.astrologers.com

Printed in the United States of America

Contents

Translator's Preface   vii

Preface to the Second Edition   xix

Preface to the Third Edition   xxi

Summary of Paul's *Introduction to Astrology*   xxiii

Paul of Alexandria: Introduction to Astrology

1. Preface   1

2. The Twelve Signs   2

3. The Terms That Were Allotted to the Five Revolving Stars In the Twelve Signs   8

4. Those Things Which the Seven Stars Have Power over from The Faces of the Decans in the Twelve Signs   10

5. The Single Degrees the Stars Rule in the Signs   12

6. The Sects of the Two Luminaries   13

7. Quadrants   14

8. Signs That See Each Other   15

9. Commanding and Obeying [Signs]   16

10. The Trine, Sextile, Square, and Opposition Aspects   17

11. Signs That Are Inconjunct with Each Other   19

12. [Signs] That Sympathize with Each Other Though Averted   20

13. Signs That Are in Aspect and Homozones and Equal-rising   21

14. The Phases That the Five Stars Make with the Sun   22

15. Stations   24

16. The Configurations That the Moon Makes with the Sun   28

17. The Separations and Applications That the Moon Makes With the Revolving Stars   30

18. Foreknowledge of the Winds   33

19. The Knowledge of How Many Are the Days of the Gods   33

20. The Knowledge of Each Day: to Which of the Gods it Belongs   34

21. The Day Ruler and the Hour Ruler   36

22. The Dodecatemories   38

23. The Seven Lots According to the *Panaretos*   41

24. Tabular Exposition of the Twelve Houses   46

25. Children   60

26. Action   62

27. Cadent Houses   63

28. The Motion of the Sun and the Rough Calculation of its Sign and Degree   65

29. The Ascendant: How it Should Be Calculated   66

30. The Midheaven   67

31. [The Ruler] of the Year, the Month, and the Day   69

32. Single-degree [Rulers] by Triplicity   71

33. Determination of the Required Degree of the Ascendant By Natural Means   73

34. Climacterics   75

35. Configuration of the Moon [With the Sun]   78

36. Rulership of the Nativity   80

37. The Nativity of the World   82

Scholia   83

Appendix I Chapter 22 of Heliodorus's Commentary   119

Index of Lots   139

Appendix II the Horoscope of Cronamon   143

Commentary   145

Index of Persons   169

Bibliography   173

Translator's Preface

I.

The available evidence points to Alexandria as the home of Classical Western astrology. The fundamental treatises of Hermes Trismegistus and Nechepso & Petosiris were presumably written there not later than the second century B.C. And, as nearly as we can judge, it was later home to a number of notable astrologers including Serapio (1st century B.C.), Claudius Ptolemy and Vettius Valens (2nd century A.D.), Paul (4th century), Hephaestio of Thebes (early 5th century), and perhaps the shadowy Rhetorius of Egypt (early 6th century). Another likely resident is the astrological poet Manetho (2nd century?). Other astrological writers who are known to us only by name may have been residents. And still others may have studied there.

Certainly, the existence of the great Alexandrian library must have facilitated the study of astrology by providing a repository for the works of succeeding generations of astrologers. We must also assume that the book shops of the city either had or could obtain copies of astrological works and the ephemerides or planetary and calendaric tables needed by astrologers. Thus, an astrologer resident in Alexandria at any time from the second century B.C. to the close of the classical era was at the heart of the living tradition and able to draw upon the accumulated knowledge of his predecessors.

History tells us that the Alexandrian population was made up in the main of three groups: Egyptians, Greeks, and Jews.[1] They didn't get along well among themselves, and jointly they constituted a volatile citizenry prone to riot. They besieged Julius Caesar when he came seeking Pompey after the battle of Pharsalus (48 B.C.). They made fun of Emperor Caracalla in 215 A.D. and suffered a grievous punishment in consequence. In the fourth century they found a new source for quarrels—the interminable Christian squabbles over the physical nature of Jesus.

Paul of Alexandria was probably born about 330 A.D.—thus, at the end of the reign of Constantine the Great. His impressionable years, from age 15 to 25, fell in the period of civil war which ensued from the three-way split of the Roman Empire among the sons of Constantine. In the east there was war with Persia (337-350). Times were hard, taxes heavy. It was a time of religious ferment, when many pagans were converting to Christianity— some out of conviction, some because the government was beginning to pass into Christian hands, and some to enjoy the privileges and opportunities that were available to Christians. Monasticism flourished, swollen by young men eager to escape military duty.

But of all this we find no reflection in Paul's *Introduction*. His book is a dispassionate exposition of the fundamentals of astrology. The turbulent times in which he lived do not intrude. He seems perfectly familiar with the astrological topics he expounds, but I think he was not a professional astrologer. Perhaps rather, someone like the Roman patrician Julius Firmicus Maternus, who had a good library of astrological authorities and a lively interest in

---

[1] In 115 the Jews of Cyrene and Cyprus staged a massive uprising, attacking their fellow-citizens of Greek origin. Many Greeks were murdered and much Greek property was destroyed or pillaged. The insurrection spread to Egypt. In 117 the emperor Trajan ordered the Roman legions into those regions and suppressed the rebellion with the usual severity. The Jewish element in Alexandria was liquidated. Thereafter, the population consisted mainly of Greeks and Egyptians.

the subject, but who confined his practice to reading the charts of family and friends.

II.

Paul's book covers the signs of the zodiac in considerable detail, and it is rich in tables for such a short work. But, like Manilius, Paul does not offer much information on the planets. There is a chapter on their phases, but none on their specific natures and significations. Nor does he discuss the fixed stars. And, when he comes to the events of life, he contents himself with the brief indications of Chapter 24 on the influences of the planets in the twelve houses. Of the individual topics of life, only those of Children and Action receive separate treatment.

As it stands, the book is incomplete. This naturally raises the question of whether Paul wrote more than we now have. And, in order to answer that, we need to know his purpose in writing the book. All we know is that he entitled it *Introduction* and that he subsequently revised it in response to some criticisms levied against it by his son Cronamon. The title implies a textbook for beginners. But a textbook should cover the fundamentals adequately. This one doesn't. Why, for example, is there no chapter devoted to the planets? And why is there a chapter on children, but none on marriage?

We cannot suppose, as some have of Manilius, that the author lacked the time to finish his book, for he says that he undertook a second edition. So, either he wrote no more than we have, or else his book has lost some chapters. We may examine the evidence. The author's preface implies that he has removed the rising times "according to the Egyptians" and substituted the more accurate rising times of Ptolemy. But he hasn't! All the rising times in the book are Egyptian. This would seem to indicate that the received text contains the preface to the second edition but the chapters of the first edition. Third, the *Commentary on Paul of Alexandria* by

Heliodorus, which covers Paul's Chapters 11-36, gives no indication of additional chapters in that part of the text (with one minor exception). And fourth, the medieval scholia relate only to the preserved text.

Embedded in Paul's Chapter 15 "Stations," which is a piece of descriptive astronomy, is a fragmentary astrological digression. This appears as a separate chapter in Heliodorus, where it is considerably expanded. It seems to me that what we have here is a fragment of an otherwise lost chapter. And, since Heliodorus in the sixth century found essentially the same text that we have, at least as regards the number and sequence of chapters, I believe that only a single defective copy of Paul's book survived into the sixth century to become the archetype of the copy used by Heliodorus and of the MSS that exist today.

I base this conclusion on the belief that Paul would have covered the missing topics in a book designed for beginners. One could argue that he wrote the book for his son, who was perhaps an only child and already married, so that chapters on brothers, parents, and marriage were unnecessary. But what about money, sickness, travel, and friends? No, I can't see any reason why Paul would have failed to treat at least those additional topics.

The curious discrepancy between what is obviously the preface to the second edition and equally obviously the text of the first edition presents another problem. The only explanation that comes to mind is that perhaps for a time both the first edition with the Egyptian rising times and the second edition with the Ptolemaic rising times were preserved together in a book container. Sometime, during the century and a half that elapsed between Paul and Heliodorus, the first edition lost its preface. Then someone wishing to carry away a copy selected the first edition, perhaps because it was less worn, and, noticing that the preface was missing, took the preface from the second edition and added it to the first edition. This hybrid copy then became the archetype.

Finally, why was this book so prized in Constantinople in the sixth century? Presumably, the scholars there had copies of many astrological books to choose from. If so, it is hard to see why Paul's little book would have become the subject of an elaborate commentary.[2] It is a good book as it goes, but it is incomplete. It hardly seems likely that it could have been in common use as a textbook. Were the library resources in the capital poorer than we might suppose, so that this was the only beginners' book available? Was it chosen because of the archaic source material it contains? Was Paul of Alexandria noteworthy in some way that we are ignorant of today? Or was the archetypal copy owned by a descendant of Paul who prized it for that reason? These questions remain unanswered.

III.

Whatever reasons the Byzantines had for their interest in Paul's *Introduction*, we value it today for its preservation of passages from the early books of astrology. In addition to his more immediate predecessors Claudius Ptolemy, Apollinaris, and Apollonius of Laodicea, Paul mentions three times "the wise men of the Egyptians" and once Trismegistus Hermes [*sic!*], who is also mentioned once in the Scholia. But he has evidently drawn most of his material from the early writers. There are several indications of this. Boll says that Paul's astrological chorography is that of Nechepso & Petosiris, which hearkens back to the world of Alexander the Great.[2] Paul's elaborate exposition of the signs of the zodiac, which takes up most of the first 13 chapters of his book, exhibits

---

[1] It has been argued that the traditional ascription of the *Commentary* to Heliodorus is incorrect and that the work was actually a series of lectures given at the University of Constantinople by Olympiodorus. Be this as it may, the question remains, why did Paul's book attract so much attention?

[2] See Boll, Franz, *Sphaera*, pp. 296-7, and the further citation by Gundel-Gundel, *Astrologumena*, p. 238. (But Bouché-Leclercq, *L'Astrologie Grecque*, pp. 345 ff., seems to think that Paul made up his own geographical distribution.)

some archaic points. And his extracts from the Hermetic works *Panaretos* and *On Climacterics* also show the same tendency. Some of this material is unique, so that despite the small compass of the *Introduction*, the book is valuable.

IV.

My principal reason for translating this book was to provide an additional source for students of Classical Western astrology. Ptolemy's *Tetrabiblos* has been available in English translation since 1701. But until now it has remained the only Greek astrological work with an English version. This has had unfortunate consequences. The great fame of Ptolemy and the lack of any other Greek astrological work in English created the false impression in astrological circles that the *Tetrabiblos* is the source of all later astrology and that it provides a complete exposition of Greek astrology.

In fact, English language astrological source material has been very restricted until recently. Manilius's *Astronomica*, Ptolemy's *Tetrabiblos*, the *Centiloquies* ascribed to Ptolemy, Hermes, and Bethen, selections from Cardan's *Seven Segments of Astrological Aphorisms*, selections from Guido Bonatti's *Introduction to the Judgments of the Stars*, Wright's translation of al-Bîrûnî's *Elements of the Art of Astrology*, and Ibn Ezra's *The Beginning of Wisdom* are about all that could be found as separate works.

The situation began to improve in 1959 with the publication of Neugebauer's and Van Hoesen's *Greek Horoscopes*, which provided no complete works, but did make nearly all the ancient horoscopes available, along with study aids and commentaries. This was followed in 1975 by Bram's translation of the *Mathesis* of Julius Firmicus Maternus, in 1976 by Pingree's English version of the Arabic Dorotheus, and in 1977 by Goold's new translation of Manilius. Pingree's translation of the *Yavanajâtaka*, which was published in 1978, is useful for comparison with the western works, and contains a valuable bibliography of Greek, Latin, Sanskrit, and Arabic astrological authors. Unfortunately, the utility of his excellent and comprehensive commentary is considerably diminished by his habit of citing his authorities in their original languages with no translations. Thus, those who read only modern European languages are left in the dark.

V.

A translation is a crutch. Ideally, the reader should have a thorough knowledge of both the language and the matter that he takes in hand. But few individuals have a perfect command of two or more languages. So the need for translations. But just as a crutch should be tailored to the needs of the user, so should a translation. And particularly the translation of a technical work with an extensive technical vocabulary peculiar to itself.

Advice is not lacking. Maimonides counsels the translator to absorb the idea he wishes to translate and to express it in his own language without regard for the forms of the original language. To do otherwise, and especially to attempt a "literal" translation, is to commit folly, he says.

Biblical translators can scarcely follow such advice, for sects and schisms have arisen over the translation of a single word! It does not seem to be sufficiently appreciated that less lofty subjects deserve similar attention. I think in most cases a translator should try to convey the semantic content of the original along with as much of the author's style as he can transform into his own language. Not an easy task. Word order must be changed. *The*'s added and subtracted. Ditto *and*'s and *but*'s. Stylistic characteristics that are common in one language but rare in another must be altered. Greek's obsession with participles is an example.

Where I have felt the need to augment the text, I have generally made my additions in brackets, although I have usually exercised the translator's prerogative to add and subtract articles and particles and repeat verbs without notice where the change improves the readability of the translation without altering its meaning.

Individual words often have overtones, and these vary considerably from one language to another. Also, some words are modern, and it would be anachronistic as well as deceptive to insert them into the translation of an ancient or medieval author. For example, the ancient astrologers sometimes describe configurations that are good, configurations that are bad, and others that are in between. It would be appropriate to use the words 'mean' or 'intermediate' to translate the Greek or Latin, but not the word 'average'. Why? The approximate meaning is satisfactory, but 'average' derives from a medieval Arabic term and also implies a mathematical operation that was unknown to the ancients. The unwary reader with no knowledge of the old languages or the state of mathematics in antiquity might suppose that the notion of an 'average' was prevalent in classical times. It wasn't.

An example from Paul. He generally uses the Greek word *astêr* 'star' where we would use "planet." I have kept his usage intact. To have translated "star" everywhere by "planet" would have given the reader the impression that Paul used the two terms the same way we do, which he did not. Astrologers know the difference between stars and planets, so there is no reason to depart from the original. On the other hand, he uses the Greek word *topos* 'place' where we would use "house." This is unacceptable today because "place" is not an astrological term, so I have translated *topos* as "house," but I have explained the difference in usage in a footnote. Likewise in the case of the Greek word *oikos* 'house'. Modern astrologers use the term "house" to refer to the celestial houses, so I have added a footnote to the first instance of the term *oikos* and thereafter translated it uniformly as "domicile."

In general, I have let older terms stand where I thought they would not cause confusion. Thus, I have translated *hypaugos* as "under the Sun beams." This term is now obsolete. Modern astrologers have lumped the three types of solar conjunctions together under the single term "combust." But the ancients were more precise than the moderns. In this and in similar cases, I return to the usage of William Lilly.

Greek had a rich vocabulary due to its fondness for compounds. Most of those present no particular problem, but some are ambiguous, and in a few cases the meaning is uncertain. Also, the Greek astrologers used some common words in specialized senses. The lexicons are not always helpful because their authors were not astrologers. I have generally added a footnote where I felt the meaning was obscure or uncertain. And in those places where I have confessed my inability to understand the Greek text, the reader who knows Greek can decide for himself whether the translator or the text is at fault.

VI.

So far as I am aware, this is the first translation of Paul's work into a modern language. The Greek text was first edited by Andreas Schato (of whom nothing is known) and published at Wittenberg in 1586, accompanied by a Latin translation. A revised edition was issued in 1588. It does not seem to have attracted much attention. I do not recall having seen any mention of it by the 17th century astrologers with whose works I am familiar.

I have used the Teubner edition (Leipzig, 1958), whose editor, the late Emilie Boer, has done an excellent job of trying to bring some order out of the diverse readings of the manuscripts. In 1962 her edition of Heliodorus's *Commentary* was published by Teubner, and it forms a valuable companion to Paul's book.

Despite Boer's best efforts, the text is not in very good shape. The MS tradition is diffuse. Some of the copyists apparently paraphrased or reworded the text to suit themselves, and, since the oldest MSS frequently disagree, recourse must be had to comparison with other Greek and Latin astrological works, to probability, and to conjecture.

The Manuscripts

I have not seen any of the MSS. The notes below are from the *Catalogus Codicum Astrologorum Graecorum* (CCAG) and from Boer's edition. There are some discrepancies among the CCAG descriptions, Boer's descriptions, and her apparatus criticus. Also, there are errors in page numbers and other details of her notes and apparatus. I have tried to resolve these as best I could without having resort to the MSS.

Paul's *Introduction* is preserved in whole or part in nearly 50 MSS. Their contents are as follows:

- 10 with all or most of the chapters
- 2 now incomplete, but perhaps once complete
- 3 copied from incomplete exemplars
- 1 nearly complete, but some chapters are abridged
- 32 with one or more chapters or parts of chapters

Only one of the MSS goes back as far as the 10th or 11th century. The others are mostly of the 15th century, with a few from the 14th. They exhibit many variants. Boer has studied their relationships and concluded that they all descend from a subarchetype of the 10/11th century, which in turn was descended from a poor archetype of perhaps the 6th century. She has postulated three family groups, β, γ, and δ, of which γ and δ derive directly from the subarchetype, while β is an offshoot of γ, and six MSS that derive independently from the subarchetype. The most important of the independent MSS are these:

L Laurentianus Graecus 28,34 ff.170 a parchment MS of the 10/11th century containing an astrological miscellany. Its text of

Paul, which is scattered through the MS, goes back to the subarchetype. Unfortunately, it contains only a few chapters (2, 3, 4, 14, and 16).

Z Parisinus Graecus 2506 ff. 276 an oriental paper MS of the beginning of the 14th century containing an astrological miscellany. It is from the library of Jean Huraut, Sieur de Boistaille (c.1510-1572), a French diplomat who was in Constantinople on official business in 1552 and who served as the French ambassador to Venice 1560-63. The text of Paul in this MS goes back to the subarchetype. It now contains Chapters 1-14 (beginning only), 20-23, 25-27 (beginning only), and 31-37 (beginning only). Paul's work appears out of sequence, with Chapter 31 on f.46^v and the others (including Chapter 31 again) scattered through ff.149-183. Of these, Chapters 20-21 appear on f.149 in a more recent hand. Boer considers this to be the best of the MSS.

Y Parisinus Graecus 2425 ff. 216 a paper MS of the 15th century from the library of Catherine de Médicis (1519-1589), Queen of France. This is the famous astrological MS which also contains Ptolemy's *Tetrabiblos* and the valuable *Summary* of a number of astrological works, including Paul's *Introduction*. It is notable for its frequent misspelling of words due to the scribe's ignorance of the classical spelling. Robbins suggests (in the preface to his translation of the *Tetrabiblos*, p. xvii) that this may indicate that the scribe copied from dictation, although Boer notes that the planetary and zodiacal symbols it uses appear to be derived from capital letters, which might indicate that it (or its exemplar) was copied from a MS written in capital letters. Boer says that the text of Paul's *Introduction* goes back to the subarchetype, although the MS sometimes omits, abridges, and rewords portions of the text in a fitful manner. She evidently assumes that the text of the *Summary*, which appears elsewhere in the MS, was copied from another exemplar and is therefore independent of the separate text of Paul.

Two other MSS that are used as the principal representatives of their classes are:

D Marcianus Gr. 303 ff.234 a paper MS of the 14/15 century. This MS is a copy of the XIV century MS Parmensis Gr. 165 which is now incomplete. It is used as a representative of the family of MSS derived from a lost MS designated as γ, whose text of Paul is presumed to have been copied from the subarchetype. Paul's *Introduction to Apotelesmatics* [*sic*] appears on ff. 221^v-241. This MS alone preserves a relatively intact text of Chapters 28-30, which otherwise are only found in a shortened and altered form in MSS **Y** and **v**.

M Marcianus Gr. 335 ff. 434 a paper MS of the XV century very neatly written; the lower margins and sometimes the lower part of the text on the leaves has been damaged by damp. It is used as a representative of the family of MSS derived from a lost MS designated as β and it alone now contains the whole text (with the exception of Chapters 28-30). Boer judges that β was copied from γ; hence, **M** usually agrees with **D**. Paul's *Introduction* appears as a single work on ff. 212^v-221, but some individual chapters are repeated elsewhere in the MS and may have been derived from other exemplars.

The *Summary* was apparently made by some unknown medieval scholar who went through the works of several astrological authors (Ptolemy, Antiochus of Athens, Paul of Alexandria, et al.) and briefly summarized their contents. Thus, the summaries are valuable because they provide a synopsis of the works (some of which are no longer extant) that is or may be independent of the MSS that have come down to us. In the case of Paul's *Introduction*, the summary corresponds closely to Boer's text; therefore, the reader may ignore it and proceed directly to the text.

I am pleased to have found the time to translate Paul's *Introduction* and to prepare it for publication. Hopefully, I may be able to produce some more translations in the future.

James H. Holden
April 16, 1986, Dallas, Texas

Preface to the Second Edition

The first edition of my translation of Paul's *Introduction* with a short Preface of two pages was completed in mid-1985. Since I had no opportunity to publish it, I circulated it privately among my friends. Feeling, however, that the Preface was inadequate, I rewrote it in April 1986.

Recently, I received a request for a copy of the translation from the eminent Italian astrologer Grazia Mirti. However, the first edition (and the original Preface) was printed on a 9-pin dot matrix printer, but the 1986 Preface was printed on a 24-pin printer. Rather than transmit a copy of the revised Preface and the translation in dissimilar formats, I have reset the entire work using a more modern word processor and printer.

At the same time, I have taken the opportunity to correct some typographical errors in the first edition and to make a thorough revision of the translation. I have also added some notes to the Scholia and indicated their points of reference in the text by a superscript S followed by a period and the number of the scholium. I have also added a Commentary that was written in 1986 but never circulated. Thus, this second edition is improved both in content and appearance. (The reader should note that the words "Second Edition" that appear below the title on p. 1 refer to Paul's second edition, not to the second edition of my translation, although in this instance they are appropriate to both.)

Having rethought the problem (see Section II of the Preface to the first edition), I would like to offer another suggestion as to why Paul's book is described as being a "second edition" when this does not appear to be the case. Perhaps a more likely possibility, is that Paul began to write a second edition but never got past the Introduction. Subsequently, the new Introduction was attached to or kept with the first edition and was substituted for the original Introduction by a copyist. But the true reason may remain unknown.

It is gratifying to note that several new translations of ancient and medieval astrological works have appeared in the 8-year interval since 1986. I hope that these translations, in company with those previously available, will help to spark a renewed interest in early astrology and to provide an improved foundation for a better understanding of this ancient art.

James H. Holden
January 8, 1994
Phoenix, Arizona

Preface to the Third Edition

The second edition was circulated privately, as was the first edition. Now at last, I have had an opportunity to publish this translation. I wish to thank Kris Brandt Riske, Executive Director of the A.F.A., for converting my word processor file into a publishing file and seeing the book through the printing process. I also want to thank Jack Cipolla, A.F.A. Operations Manager, for designing the covers. The main text of this third edition is little changed from that of the second edition. However, I have corrected some typographical errors and made a few minor revisions in the translation.

The major change is the addition of Appendix I, in which I have given a translation of Chapter 22 of the sixth century *Commentary on Paul of Alexandria* by Heliodorus (or, Olympiodorus, as some will have it). Chapter 22 of that work contains the most extensive listing of Lots that has come down to us in Greek. Whether they derive from earlier Greek sources,[1] or even in part from a Greek translation of one of Albumasar's Arabic works, is unknown. At any rate, this listing of 98 Lots may indicate that the term "Arabic Parts" is at least to some extent a misnomer. For the convenience of the reader, I have added an Index of Lots to those in that Appendix, showing the page number on which the formula for the Lot is mentioned.

---

[1] We must remember that Julius Firmicus Maternus's *Mathesis*, much of which was translated from Greek sources, contains some 20 Lots, so at least that many were already known in the Classical period.

Since I completed work on the second edition in 1993, I have learned of two other translations of Paul's book that were published in that same year, one into English and the other into Italian, and a still later one that was published in 2002. I have not seen any of them.

Paulus Alexandrinus
Introductory Matters.
trans. by Robert Schmidt
Berkeley Springs, W. Va.: Golden Hind Press, 1993.

Paolo d'Alessandria
Lineamenti introduttivi alla scienza
della previsione astronomica.
[Introductory Outlines to the Science
of Astronomical Prediction]
trans. into Italian by Giuseppe Bezza
Milan, 1993.

Late Classical Astrology:
Paulus Alexandrinus & Olympiodorus
with the Scholia from later commentators.
trans. by Dorian Gieseler Greenbaum, M.A.
Reston, Virginia: ARHAT Publications, 2002

James H. Holden
July 26, 2010
Phoenix, Arizona

Summary of Paul's
Introduction

Paul teaches in his *Introduction* that each of the 12 signs has 3 decans, 30 degrees, [and] 60 minutes, and that Aries [is] the beginning of the zodiacal circle; which of the signs are said to be masculine and which feminine, which tropical and which fixed and which bicorporeal, and of what kind [are the] equinoctial and the vernal, and which [are] of summer, and of what kind [are those] of autumn and those of winter.

Furthermore, of which of the signs it is said [that it is] the house or the exaltation or the fall of some one of the planets, and which of the [bodily] parts of man each of the signs rules, and in which clime it is situated, and to which wind it was allotted; how many also and which of the signs are a triplicity; and that Aries and Leo and Sagittarius by day are the triplicity of the Sun, but by night of Jupiter; Taurus and Virgo and Capricorn [are] by day the triplicity of Venus, but by night of the Moon; Gemini and Libra and Aquarius [are] by day the triplicity of Saturn, but by night of Mercury; and Cancer and Scorpio and Pisces by day of Venus, but by night of Mars; and towards which of the winds each of the triplicities is assigned; and to which country each of the signs is attached; and in how many hours each rises in the clime of Alexandria; and what are the terms of each of the 5 planets, for the Sun and the Moon have no terms; and that from the inspection of the terms the Egyptians seek after the years of life; and that the decans are said to be "faces" of the 7 stars; and that again each of the 7 rules over its own degrees in any one of the signs; also, what is the sect and what [is] the *doryphory*; also, which [is] diurnal, which nocturnal, which occidental; and how many of the 4 quadrants [are] masculine, how many feminine; and which of these [are] rising and eastern, which southern and meridional, and simply, which are made familiar to which winds; and how many times is each of these 4 visible.

Furthermore, he explains which of the signs are said to be beholding each other, and which commanding, and which hearing, and with which each of them is well disposed; also, of which ones the trine aspect composes [its] sides, of which ones the square, and of which ones the sextile, and what is more the opposition of which ones; what force each of these said aspects has; and that the signs [that are] configured according to none of these aspects are called "averted" and "disjunct;" and what the stars declare when they are in these [configurations]; also, which of these averted [signs] are called "*homozones*," which "equal rising," and which "neighboring;" and how many of them are called "arranged on the right;" and with which of these each one shares its power; and that the planets Saturn and Jupiter and Mars are said to "attend," and why; and when the five planets are said to be matutine or conjunct (the Sun); and that their attendances around the Sun are [so] termed according to the preceding degrees and the preceding signs; but the attendances around the Moon whenever they are found in the same sign and whenever in the following; what too is "stationary" and what is "adding to the numbers" ["direct"], and what is "retrograde," and how the station comes about and when and how often; and when [they are] in opposition (to the Sun) and why; and what each of these configurations shows; and that [there are] 11 configurations of the Moon, which are also called "phases;" and that the full Moon is also called the "full moon conjunction"; what too is termed "waning," and why each of these configurations of the Moon received the nomenclature appropriate to it; what too is "separation" and "application," and that from these the foreknowledge of the winds is sought out; and the protraction and also the brevity of the sicknesses and the life of men is sought out from the topic of separation and application.

But in addition, according to another conception, what is termed "to preside over" the same and "to manage," and what is termed with reference to the stars in the one case to preside and in the other to manage, and of what things these are indicative, and that the one presiding and the one managing is also termed lord of the day.[1]

And that Saturn was allotted the first zone of the seven zones, being very cold and lying in the frost; the [star] of Jupiter the second, being temperate and nourishing and life-producing; the [star] of Mars the third, [being] fiery and destructive; the [star] of the Sun the fourth and middle, being fiery and life-producing; Venus the fifth, [being] mild, who is also the cause of conception and offspring; Mercury the sixth, being moist; the Moon the seventh, it too being moist.

How one must get the *dodecatemory* of the seven stars and each of the four angles and the Lot [of Fortune], which degrees it has, and what each of these shows; and what [is] the Lot of Fortune and how it is sought out; and what [is] the [Lot] of the Daemon and of Love and of Boldness and of Necessity and of Victory and of Retribution; and what [is] the "Basis" and what forces each of these exhibits. But also, what [is] the Lot of the Father, what of the Mother and of Brothers and of Children and of the Wife and also how each of these is obtained.

[Also a chapter] on the tabular examination of the twelve houses; and that the beginning of these [is] the ASC, which is also called "tiller" and "basis." Second is the so-called Livelihood, which is also termed the Gate of Hades and the succedent of the ASC; and third in order the so-called God, being the house of the

---

[1]The star that "presides" is the planetary day-ruler, while the star that "manages" is the ruler of the planetary hour.

Moon and being called the Good Cadent; and the rest one after the other down to the twelfth. And what order they received; and what they show, each of these playing host to the benefics of the planets or the malefics.

The investigation [of the topic] of children is found; and from what stars the topic of action is sought out and from what houses, a detailed explanation of cadent houses, and when these become effective; and what [is the method] of getting the place of the Sun approximately and of getting the year and month and day for a nativity, [and] how from the subdivision of these same into *dodecatemories* it is easy to find in which sign is the year which is sought and also similarly the month and the day; how one must calculate the ASC and how the MC[1]; and how the single degree division is got, and that the Egyptians proposed it as useful for obtaining the ASC to the [very] degree; and that five[2] [different] opinions about this were produced; and that the ascending degree of the day favorable for birth is termed "delivery;" and besides this, in the case of climacterics, which of them are inevitable, and which are moderate, and which are avoidable.

All of these things Paul expounds—none worse than the others—and besides this, the conjunction of the Moon.

---

[1] The text of MS **Y** has *mesembria* 'southern', by which is meant *mesouranema* 'MC'.
[2] Cumont points out that the text of Chapter 33 offers only three methods.

Paul of Alexandria

Introduction to Astrology

Second Edition

1. *PREFACE.*

Quite correctly, my dear son Cronamon, when you discovered our erroneous statements in the previous edition, you urged us to compile another that would be lacking in none of the principles contributing to its exposition, also necessarily taking into account the rising times according to Ptolemy for explaining the astrological indications, since we have found these to be more serviceable, and since Ptolemy himself in his [chapter on] "The Length of Life"[1] makes use of them, and Apollinarius[2] in his *The Apheta and the Ruler and the Anaereta* recommends that we use them; in addition to which, Apollonius of Laodicea[3] in his five books charges

---

[1] *Tetrabiblos*, iii. 10 (Robbins's edition in the Loeb Classical Library).
[2] An early astrological writer also cited by Vettius Valens, *Anthology*, vi. 4, and possibly in ix. 12. Hence, he must have lived in the 2nd century A.D. or earlier. Note that he is said to have recommended the use of the rising times according to Ptolemy. At first glance, this would seem to mean that he wrote after Ptolemy. But there is a possibility that "Ptolemy's rising times" were actually copied from those of an earlier writer and that Apollinarius used those. Valens, who lived in Alexandria during Ptolemy's liftetime, mentions Apollinarius, but he does not use Ptolemy's rising times. And there is good reason to believe that Ptolemy's tables were not available to the public until the end of the 3rd century. I believe the next mention of Apollinarius after Paul is by Hephaestio of Thebes, who lived in the early 5th century. So there is a problem here.
[3] Otherwise unknown.

the Egyptians with having perpetrated much fraud in [their statement of] the rising times of the signs.[1]

2. *THE TWELVE SIGNS.*

The zodiacal circle moves obliquely, being divided into twelve
sections that are called *signs*. A sign has 3 decans and 30 degrees,
and a degree has 60 minutes.

The beginning of the zodiacal circle is Aries, masculine, equinoctial, tropical, vernal, domicile[2] of Mars, exaltation of the Sun
around 19 degrees, fall of Saturn around 20 degrees; triplicity by
day of the Sun, and by night of Jupiter. It lies in the clime of Persia,
having been assigned to *Apeliotes* (the East Wind). It rules the
head and all of the face. The sign rises according to the Egyptians
in the Third Clime from the invisible part of the world into the visible in 1 1/3 1/9 equinoctial hours (1:26:40) or 21 2/3 times
(21°40').[3] The MC angle of the Horoscope of the World is in this
sign.[4]

[1]Paul refers to the fact that the traditional rising times differed signifi-
cantly from the accurately calculated times given by Ptolemy. Here are
the rising times for the first six signs "according to the Egyptians" with
the Ptolemaic times for the third Clime in parentheses: Aries 21°40'
(20°53'), Taurus 25°00' (24°12), Gemini 28°20' (29°55'), Cancer 31°40'
(34°37'), Leo 35°00' (35°36'), Virgo 38°20' (34°47'). See the
Commentary.
[2]The Greek term is *oikos* 'house'; however, to avoid confusion with the
celestial houses, I shall translate this word as 'domicile'.
[3]Paul follows the Egyptian practice of giving the figures in integer hours
and times and (mostly) unit fractions. I have inserted in parentheses the
equivalent hours, minutes, and seconds of time and the equivalent degrees and minutes of arc. An *equinoctial time* is 4 minutes or 1 degree of
sidereal time. Despite Cronamon's complaint, these are the rising times
"according to the Egyptians" rather than the more exact ones given by
Ptolemy. Thus, it would appear that despite the explicit statement that
this is the second edition of the work, the Ptolemaic rising times are not
given. See the Translator's Preface for a discussion of this matter.
[4]This refers to the Horoscope of the World itself, which, in the
Sign-House system has the MC in Aries and the ASC in Cancer. See
Chapter 37 for the planetary placements.

The second sign is Taurus, feminine, fixed, vernal, domicile of Venus, exaltation of the Moon around 3 degrees, fall of none; triplicity by day of Venus, and by night of the Moon. It lies in the clime of Babylonia, having been assigned to *Notos* (the South Wind). It rules the neck and tendons. The sign rises from the invisible into the visible part of the world in 1 2/3 hours (1:40:00) or 25 times (25°00′) in the clime mentioned.

The third sign is Gemini, masculine, bicorporeal, vernal, human, domicile of Mercury, exaltation of none, fall of none; triplicity by day of Saturn, and by night of Mercury. It lies in the clime of Cappadocia, having been assigned to *Lips* (the Southwest Wind). It rules the shoulders, the arms and hands, and the fingers. The sign rises from the invisible into the visible part of the world in 1 2/3 1/5 1/45 hours (1:53:20) or 28 1/3 times (28°20′) in the clime mentioned. The season of spring is completed in this quadrant, whence it is called "air."[1]

The fourth sign is Cancer, feminine, tropical, aestival, domicile of the Moon, exaltation of Jupiter around 15 degrees, fall of Mars around 28 degrees; triplicity by day of Venus, and by night of Mars. It lies in the clime of Armenia, having been assigned to *Borras* (the North Wind). The sign rises from the invisible into the visible part of the world in 2 1/9 hours (2:06:40) or 31 2/3 times (31°40′) in the clime mentioned. The ASC of the World is in this sign.

The fifth sign is Leo, masculine, fixed, aestival, domicile of the Sun, exaltation of none, fall of none; triplicity by day of the Sun, and by night of Jupiter. It lies in the clime of Asia, having been assigned to *Apeliotes* (the East Wind). It rules the ribs. The sign rises from the invisible into the visible part of the world in 2 1/3 hours (2:20:00) or 35 times (35°00′) in the clime mentioned.

---

[1]Note that the four seasons are assigned to the four elements in the sequence air, fire, earth, water.

The sixth sign is Virgo, feminine, bicorporeal, aestival, domicile and exaltation of Mercury around the 15th degree, fall of Venus around 27 degrees; triplicity by day of Venus, and by night of the Moon. It lies in the clime of Greece and Ionia, having been assigned to *Notos* (the South Wind). It rules the loins and the upper intestines and all the insides. The sign rises from the invisible into the visible part of the world in 2 1/3 1/5 1/45 hours (2:33:20) or 38 1/3 times (38;20). The season of summer is completed in this quadrant, whence it is called "fire."

The seventh sign is Libra, masculine, equinoctial, tropical, autumnal, domicile of Venus, exaltation of Saturn around 20 degrees, fall of the Sun around 19 degrees; triplicity by day of Saturn, and by night of Mercury. It lies in the clime of Libya and Cyrene, having been assigned to *Lips* (the Southwest Wind). It rules the hips and the buttocks. The sign rises from the invisible into the visible part of the world in 2 1/3 1/5 1/45 hours (2:33:20) or 38 1/3 times (38;20). The IMC of the World is in this sign.

The eighth sign is Scorpio, feminine, fixed, autumnal, domicile of Mars, exaltation of none, fall of the Moon around 3 degrees; triplicity by day of Venus, and by night of Mars. It lies in the clime of Italy, having been assigned to *Borras* (the North Wind). It rules the genitals, the bladder, and the groin. The sign rises from the invisible into the visible part of the world in 2 1/3 hours (2:20:00) or 35 times (35°00′).

The ninth sign is Sagittarius, masculine, bicorporeal, autumnal, domicile of Jupiter, exaltation of none, fall of none; triplicity by day of the Sun, and by night of Jupiter. It lies in the clime of Cilicia and Crete, having been assigned to *Apeliotes* (the East Wind). It rules the thighs. The sign rises from the invisible into the visible part of the world in 2 1/9 hours (2:06:40) or 31 2\3 times (31°40′) in the clime mentioned. The season of autumn is completed in this quadrant, whence it is called "earth."

The tenth sign is Capricorn, feminine, tropical, hibernal, domicile of Saturn, exaltation of Mars around 28 degrees, fall of Jupiter around 15 degrees; triplicity by day of Venus, and by night of the Moon. It lies in the clime of Syria, having been assigned to *Notos* (the South Wind). It rules the knees. The sign rises from the invisible into the visible part of the world in 1 2/3 1/5 1/45 hours (1:53:20) or 28 1/3 times (28°20′). It is the DSC of the World.

The eleventh sign is Aquarius, masculine, fixed, hibernal, domicile of Saturn, exaltation of none, fall of none; triplicity by day of Saturn, and by night of Mercury. It lies in the clime of Egypt, having been assigned to *Lips* (the Southwest Wind). It rules the lower legs. The sign rises from the invisible into the visible part of the world in 1 2/3 hours (1:40:00) or 25 times (25°00′).

The twelfth sign is Pisces, feminine, bicorporeal, hibernal, domicile of Jupiter, exaltation of Venus around 27 degrees, fall of Mercury around 15 degrees; triplicity by day of Venus, and by night of Mars. It lies in the clime of the Red Sea and the land of India, having been assigned to *Borras* (the North Wind). It rules the soles of the feet and the feet in general. The sign rises from the invisible into the visible part of the world in 1 1/3 1/9 hours (1:26:40) or 21 2/3 times (21°40′). The season of winter is completed in this quadrant, whence it is called "water."

And, as regards the sequential exposition of the twelve [signs], let this suffice, but as regards their collective signification, let it be set forth as follows.[1]

The masculine signs are these—Aries, Gemini, Leo, Libra, Sagittarius, and Aquarius; those remaining are feminine—Taurus,

---

[1] Georg Gundel thinks the short paragraphs that follow are memory-aids; but Boer thinks they may have been excerpts from the preceding text that were first written in the margin and eventually added to the end of the text. She points out some discrepancies in the order of these paragraphs and the abundance of variant readings in the MSS. The CCAG contains some other texts that are similar.

Cancer, Virgo, Scorpio, Capricorn, and Pisces. And speaking generally, those that are odd-numbered, counting from the first sign Aries, are to be considered masculine, and those that are even, feminine.

The tropical signs[1] are Aries, Cancer, Libra, and Capricorn. The equinoctial signs are Aries and Libra. Equal in number to the tropicals are the fixed signs Taurus, Leo, Scorpio, and Aquarius. And equal in number to these are the bicorporeal signs,[S.1] which are Gemini, Virgo, Sagittarius, and Pisces. And in sum, those signs that make up the groups of four receive the same nature.

Domiciles. Aries and Scorpio [are the domiciles] of Mars, Taurus and Libra of Venus, Gemini and Virgo of Mercury, Cancer of the Moon, Leo of the Sun, Sagittarius and Pisces of Jupiter, Capricorn and Aquarius of Saturn.

Exaltations. Aries [is the exaltation] of the Sun, Taurus of the Moon, Cancer of Jupiter, Virgo of Mercury, Libra of Saturn, Capricorn of Mars, Pisces of Venus. And those [signs] that are separated from these by an interval of seven signs[2] are the falls.

Triplicities. Aries, Leo, [and] Sagittarius [are ruled] by day by the Sun, by night by Jupiter; Taurus, Virgo, [and] Capricorn by day by Venus, by night by the Moon; Gemini, Libra, [and] Aquarius by day by Saturn, by night by Mercury; Cancer, Scorpio, [and] Pisces by day by Venus, by night by Mars.

The first triplicity is assigned to *Apeliotes* (the East Wind), the second to *Notos* (the South Wind), the third to *Lips* (the Southwest Wind), the fourth to *Borras* (the North Wind).

---

[1] Cardinal signs in modern terminology.
[2] Contrary to the modern custom, the ancients counted both ends of a sequence to determine the interval; hence, "seven signs" to Paul is "six signs" or 180 degrees to us. He is referring to the opposite sign.

The signs have an affinity for certain countries: Aries for Persia, Taurus for Babylon, Gemini for Cappadocia, Cancer for Armenia, Leo for Asia, Virgo for Greece, Libra for Libya, Scorpio for Italy, Sagittarius for Crete, with Capricorn having been allotted to Syria, Aquarius receiving Egypt, [and] Pisces being assigned to the country of India.[1] [S.2]

Of the parts of the human body, Aries has an affinity for the head; Taurus rules the neck; Gemini portrays the shoulders and upper arms; Cancer being allotted to the chest; Leo has the stomach and the ribs, Virgo the [parts] below the belly; Libra rules the buttocks; Scorpio has the secret [parts], Sagittarius the thighs, Capricorn the knees, Aquarius the shins, [and] Pisces the feet.[2]

According to the Egyptians,[3] each of these signs rises in the third clime, which is that of Alexandria, [as follows]: Aries and Pisces in 1 1/3 1/9 hours (1:26:40) or 21 2/3 times (21°40′), Taurus and Aquarius in 1 2/3 hours (1:40:00) or 25 times (25°00′), Gemini and Capricorn in 1 2/3 1/5 1/45 hours (1:53:20) or 28 1/3 times (28°20′), Cancer and Sagittarius in 2 1/9 hours (2:06:40) or 31 2/3 times (31°40′), Leo and Scorpio in 2 1/3 hours (2:20:00) or 35 times (35°00′), Virgo and Libra in 2 1/3 1/5 1/45 hours (2:33:20) or 38 1/3 times (38°20′).[4]

---

[1] These geographical assignments agree with the ones in the earlier part of the chapter, but fewer regions are mentioned here.
[2] The parts of the body assigned to the individual signs do not always agree with those mentioned in the earlier part of this chapter, e.g. here we have the stomach assigned to Leo, but above it is assigned to Cancer. And in general, fewer body parts are mentioned here than above.
[3] The numbers that follow first appear in Hypsicles, *Anaphorikos* 'Ascension'. Hypsicles was a Greek mathematician who flourished in the early part of the second century B.C. His book explains the theory of calculating rising times by arithmetical progression, a method originated by the Babylonians, and he gives explicit calculations for the clime of Alexandria. See the Commentary for a detailed discussion.
[4] Here, as previously, Paul gives the rising times in hours and fractional parts of an hour, e.g. '1 1/3 1/9 hour' rather than '1:26:40 hours'. Similarly, for the horary times.

3. *THE TERMS THAT WERE ALLOTTED TO THE FIVE REVOLVING STARS IN THE TWELVE SIGNS*[1]

The lengths [in degrees] that are divided among the five planets within the 30 degrees of the signs are called *terms*.[2] Terms are not assigned to the Sun and the Moon, for these [luminaries] out of preference also divided the domiciles among the five planets.[S.3] For, a star rejoices, as it were, in the sign of its own triplicity or in its domicile or its exaltation, thus also in its own terms in each sign. They have the order in tabular exhibition as is written next below.

Exhibition of the Terms[S.4] According to Signs and Stars.[S.5]

Aries	Taurus	Gemini	Cancer	Leo	Virgo
♃ 6 6	♀ 8 8	☿ 6 6	♂ 7 7	♃ 6 6	☿ 7 7
♀ 6 12	☿ 6 14	♃ 6 12	♀ 6 13	♀ 5 11	♀ 10 17
☿ 8 20	♃ 8 22	♀ 5 17	☿ 6 19	♄ 7 18	♃ 4 21
♂ 5 25	♄ 5 27	♂ 7 24	♃ 7 26	☿ 6 24	♂ 7 28
♄ 5 30	♂ 3 30	♄ 6 30	♄ 4 30	♂ 6 30	♄ 2 30

Libra	Scorpio	Sagitt.	Capric.	Aquar.	Pisces
♄ 6 6	♂ 7 7	♃ 12 12	☿ 7 7	☿ 7 7	♀ 12 12
☿ 8 14	♀ 4 11	♀ 5 17	♃ 7 14	♀ 6 13	♃ 4 16
♃ 7 21	☿ 8 19	☿ 4 21	♀ 8 22	♃ 7 20	☿ 3 19
♀ 7 28	♃ 5 24	♄ 5 26	♄ 4 26	♂ 5 25	♂ 9 28
♂ 2 30	♄ 6 30	♂ 4 30	♂ 4 30	♄ 5 30	♄ 2 30
♄ 57	♃ 79	♂ 66	♀ 82	☿ 76	360

---

[1]Boer deletes the words 'because when they are found in these degrees they rejoice just as they do in their own signs' which follow the title.
[2]The Greek word is *horia* 'boundaries'. The Latin equivalent is *termini*, from which our English word *terms* is taken. Note that the *terms* were the boundaries between the *lengths* or *extents* within each sign that were assigned to the five planets. Thus, we say properly that some point in the zodiac is "in the *terms*" of a certain planet, meaning that it is "within the boundaries" of the extent of degrees that is assigned to that planet.

For by means of these same the wise men of the Egyptians judged the matter of the Ruler of the Nativity[1] [S.6] from which also the [matter] of the length of life[S.7] is determined. For also, by analogy with the aggregation of the 360 degrees of the zodiacal circle, the number of the terms was completed by the summation of the *terms*, of which each of the stars was allotted a number in each sign—the summation giving the full years of the life, e.g. for Saturn 57 years, for Jupiter 79 years, Mars 66 years, Venus 82 years, Mercury 76 years.[2] And we have made for ourselves a table of the quantity of the *terms* which the stars have in the whole zodiac.

But someone will ask for what reason the Sun and the Moon became foreign to the rulership of the *terms*. In response to which, this can be said: they rule everything, and, being kings of all things, they obtained dominion over all things overwhelmingly; and if indeed in a nativity the Sun is found [to be] the one chosen [as ruler] of the length of life and, being well situated, is effective with regard to its dominion, he gives the full years of life [as] 120. But when the Moon is found according to the foregoing mode, if she is found effective in the matter of life, she gives the full years of life [as] 108.

---

[1] Literally 'house-rulership' but here referring to rulership of the nativity, or, more precisely, to the selection of the planet that represents the life of the native—what Firmicus calls the 'giver of life'. The selection depends in part on counting the number of dignities a planet possesses, and being in its own *terms* is a dignity. Note that the terms 'house-rulership' and 'house-ruler' are used in various senses. The 'house-ruler' is literally the ruler of a sign, but the term is often extended to mean 'significator' or even, as here, 'Ruler of the Nativity'.

[2] That is, if a particular planet is judged to be the significator of the length of life, then the maximum years that might be expected correspond to the sums of the degrees within its *terms*. See the note at the end of the table below.

Signs	Quantity of Terms		Quantity of Terms		Quantity of Terms		Quantity of Terms		Quantity of Terms	
Aries	5	[S.8]5	6	6	5	5	6	6	8	8
Taurus	5	10	8	14	3	8	8	14	6	14
Gemini	6	16	6	20	7	15	5	19	6	20
Cancer	4	20	7	27	7	22	6	25	6	26
Leo	7	27	6	33	6	28	5	30	6	32
Virgo	2	29	4	37	7	35	10	40	7	39
Libra	6	35	7	44	2	37	7	47	8	47
Scorpio	6	41	5	49	7	44	4	51	8	55
Sagitt.	5	46	12	61	4	48	5	56	4	59
Capric.	4	50	7	68	4	52	8	64	7	66
Aquar.	5	55	7	75	5	57	6	70	7	73
Pisces	2	57	4	79	9	66	12	82	3	76
total 360	the terms of Saturn give years of life 57		the terms of Jupiter give years of life 79		the terms of Mars give years of life 66		the terms of Venus give years of life 82		the terms of Mercury give years of life 76	

They become givers of these years whenever in a nativity, being well and properly effective, they are allotted the condition of rulership.

4. THOSE THINGS WHICH THE SEVEN STARS HAVE POWER OVER FROM THE FACES OF THE DECANS IN THE TWELVE SIGNS. [S.9-13]

The *faces* of the seven stars [which are distributed] through the signs [and which arise] from the shaping [done] by the *decans*,[1] in

---

[1] The Eyptians regarded the *decans* proper as gods who had power over the zodiac and the seven planets, and through them over "all events that befall men collectively" (Scott's translation). See W. Scott, *Hermetica* (Oxford: The Clarendon Press, 1924), vol. 1, 411-419, Stobaeus's 6th excerpt *From the Discourses of Hermes to Tat*, and Scott's commentary in vol. 2, 363-386 (diagram on p. 374).

which the stars rejoice just as though (they were) in their own domiciles, must be worked out in the same order as the *heptazone*,[1] from which the ruler of the day and the ruler of the hour are got, making the beginning from Aries and including 10 degrees for each one up to the required star. I mean, always giving the first *decan* to Mars, the second to the Sun (according to the order of the ruler of the day and the ruler of the hour), and the third to Venus; then, in order, in Taurus, the first must be given to the star of Mercury, then to the Moon, then to Saturn; but in Gemini, the first to Jupiter, the second to Mars, and the third to the Sun; and in order as the rest of them come in accordance with their number in the *heptazone*. But for finding the *face* of the required star quickly, we have made a tabular exposition of them as is written below.

The Faces of the Signs.

Aries		*Taurus*		*Gemini*		*Cancer*		*Leo*		*Virgo*	
faces	dg	faces	dg	faces	dg	faces	dg	faces	dg	faces	dg
♂	10	☿	10	♃	10	♀	10	♄	10	☉	10
☉	20	☽	20	♂	20	☿	20	♃	20	♀	20
♀	30	♄	30	☉	30	☽	30	♂	30	☿	30

Libra		*Scorpio*		*Sagitt.*		*Capric.*		*Aquar.*		*Pisces*	
faces	dg	faces	dg	faces	dg	faces	dg	faces	dg	faces	dg
☽	10	♂	10	☿	10	♃	10	♀	10	♄	10
♄	20	☉	20	☽	20	♂	20	☿	20	♃	20
♃	30	♀	30	♄	30	☉	30	☽	30	♂	30

---

[1]*Heptazone* is the Greek name for the sequence of the seven planets that puts them in the order of their mean motions, viz. Saturn, Jupiter, Mars, Sun, Venus, Mercury, Moon. This is the sequence of the planetary hours, which in turn produces the sequence Sun, Moon, Mars, Mercury, Jupiter, Venus, Saturn for the days of the week. It goes back at least to the first century B.C. and is perhaps a century older than that.

5. *THE SINGLE DEGREES THAT THE STARS RULE IN THE SIGNS.*

The single degree[1] division of the stars must be distributed following their position in the *heptazone*, assigning the first degree to that star whose sign it is, but the second to the one after it in the order of the *heptazone*, and so on until you come down to the degree which the star holds, including the minutes as one degree.[2] [S.14] We have subjoined a tabular diagram of these.

Table of the Single Degree Division.[S.15]

Deg.	♈ ♏	♉ ♎	♊ ♍	♋	♌	♐ ♓	♑ ♒
1	♂	♀	☿	☽	☉	♃	♄
2	☉	☿	☽	♄	♀	♂	♃
3	♀	☽	♄	♃	☿	☉	♂
4	☿	♄	♃	♂	☽	♀	☉
5	☽	♃	♂	☉	♄	☿	♀
6	♄	♂	☉	♀	♃	☽	☿
7	♃	☉	♀	☿	♂	♄	☽
8	♂	♀	☿	☽	☉	♃	♄
9	☉	☿	☽	♄	♀	♂	♃
10	♀	☽	♄	♃	☿	☉	♂
11	☿	♄	♃	♂	☽	♀	☉
12	☽	♃	♂	☉	♄	☿	♀

[1] The Greek word is *monomoiria*, which is sometimes encountered in the modern astrological literature.

[2] That is, when the position of the star is given to degrees and minutes, the number of the degree it is in is equal to the degrees + 1. For example, a star in 13°15′ would be in the 13 + 1 = 14th degree. It is interesting to note that this sort of instruction is still necessary for astrologers, since some of them merely drop the minutes and count degrees from 0 to 29 as the Babylonians did (although, since the Babylonians had no zero, they actually counted from 1 through 2, etc., up to 30), while others round off the precise position to the nearest whole degree, both of which are illogical procedures.

13	♄	♂	☉	♀	♃	☽	☿
14	♃	☉	♀	☿	♂	♄	☽
15	♂	♀	☿	☽	☉	♃	♄
16	☉	☿	☽	♄	♀	♂	♃
17	♀	☽	♄	♃	☿	☉	♂
18	☿	♄	♃	♂	☽	♀	☉
19	☽	♃	♂	☉	♄	☿	♀
20	♄	♂	☉	♀	♃	☽	☿
21	♃	☉	♀	☿	♂	♄	☽
22	♂	♀	☿	☽	☉	♃	♄
23	☉	☿	☽	♄	♀	♂	♃
24	♀	☽	♄	♃	☿	☉	♂
25	☿	♄	♃	♂	☽	♀	☉
26	☽	♃	♂	☉	♄	☿	♀
27	♄	♂	☉	♀	♃	☽	☿
28	♃	☉	♀	☿	♂	♄	☽
29	♂	♀	☿	☽	☉	♃	♄
30	☉	☿	☽	♄	♀	♂	♃

6. *THE SECTS OF THE TWO LUMINARIES.*

Since everything is administered by the Sun and Moon, and none of the things existing in the world is produced without the rulership of these stars, it is necessary to explain the solar and lunar *sects*—what they were allotted, and that through these [*sects*] all things were created. The Sun then was allotted the day and the morning appearance[1] and the masculine signs; and it has [as its]

---

[1]The Greek word is *anatolê*, which normally means 'rising', but as it is used here it simply means 'appearance above the horizon' without reference to the direction of motion. I have therefore translated it as 'appearance', since, while 'morning rising' aptly describes the morning appearance, 'evening rising' seems to imply that when the Moon is in the west, its attendants are rising in the east, which is not the case.

doryphories[1] the [star] of Saturn and the [star] of Jupiter. But the Moon [was allotted] the night and the evening appearance and the feminine signs; and it has [as its] *doryphories* the [star] of Mars and the star of Venus, while the [star] of Mercury is common as regards its nature and rejoices with the Sun in its morning appearance but with the Moon in its evening [appearance]. For indeed, this star, since it was allotted a common nature, appears good with benefic stars but malevolent with the destructive ones.

And the benefic stars are Jupiter and Venus, but the malefics are Saturn and Mars because of their excess—the star of Saturn having a colder nature, but the [star] of Mars one that is most exceedingly fiery, while the [star] of Mercury is common as regards its nature. And in diurnal nativities the Sun and Saturn and Jupiter rejoice in masculine signs, when they are operative in good houses, but in particular Saturn and Jupiter rejoice when they are in their morning appearance; but in nocturnal [nativities] the Moon, Mars, [and] Venus rejoice when they are [in their] evening appearance and possessing feminine signs, while the latter two stars are posited in *doryphory* with the Moon.

7. QUADRANTS.

The [first] quadrant is masculine [extending] from the ascending degree up to the MC [degree]; and this quadrant is also oriental, and it is called eastern. This signifies the first age of life, I mean that of youth. The second is feminine from the MC degree down to the DSC[2] [degree]. It is southern and like mid-day. It signifies the

---

[1] 'Attendants'. The Greek word *doryphory* ('spear-bearer') means 'bodyguard for an important person' or simply 'attendant of an important person'. An analogy would be the personal attendants of a King (Sun) or a Queen (Moon). As an astrological term it refers to the planets that accompany the Sun or the Moon, especially those that rise before the Sun in the morning and those that appear with the Moon in the evening. But here it refers instead to the planets which sympathize by nature with one or the other Light and are therefore considered to be part of its sect. Note that 'attendance' is variously defined by the classical astrologers.
[2] The *dysis* 'setting' is the descendant or DSC in modern terminology.

age of life after youth, namely the middle age. The third quadrant, from the DSC degree down to the IMC,[1] is masculine, meaning "western," [and it is] called "westerly." It signifies the age of old age. The fourth quadrant, from the IMC [degree] to the ASC degree, is feminine and northern. It signifies extreme old age up to the final end of death.[2]

To understand what has just been said by means of the succession of the four quadrants, it goes like this. From the ASC degree to the IMC is the quadrant towards the North; from the IMC degree to the DSC is the one towards the West; from the DSC degree to the MC is the quadrant towards the mid-day, which signifies the [regions] towards the South; from the MC degree to the ASC is the quadrant towards the East, which signifies the [regions] towards the orient.

8. *SIGNS THAT SEE EACH OTHER.*

Seeing.

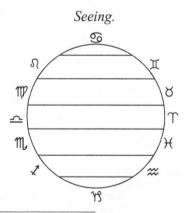

---

[1]The *hypogeion* 'under earth' is the IMC.
[2]These characterizations of the four quadrants are based upon the diurnal motion of the Sun. The day begins when the Sun comes to the ASC; and the morning is usually considered to be preliminary to the main part of the day, during which the Sun moves from the MC to the DSC; the day fades away into evening when the Sun drops below the DSC and moves toward the IMC. But other writers put death and burial at the IMC and reserve the 4th quadrant (IMC to ASC) for "the things that happen after death."

The signs that see each other are as follows: [S.16] Gemini sees Leo, and Leo looks at Gemini; Taurus sees Virgo; Aries sees Libra with an attack of guilt; Scorpio sees Pisces, and is seen by it; Aquarius looks at Sagittarius, and Sagittarius also sees Aquarius.[1] The signs that see each other are united by sympathy and affection and good will, as of a man for a woman and of a woman for a man, of a father for his children and of children for their father, of brothers for brothers, and of friends for neighbors and comradeship, and of slaves for their masters. Also, it agrees with all [types of] association and [situations] resembling these.[2]

9. COMMANDING AND OBEYING [SIGNS].

The commanding [signs] have this arrangement: Taurus commands Pisces, and Pisces obeys it; Gemini [commands] Aquarius, Cancer Capricorn, Leo Sagittarius, [and] Virgo Scorpio.[3] The

---

[1] These are the pairs of signs that are equidistant from the summer *solstice*. The earliest Alexandrian astrologers customarily reckoned by whole *signs*; hence, the entire *sign* of Cancer constituted the *solstice*. These same pairings of signs are given by Manilius, *Astronomica*, 2.485-519; Hephaestio, *Apotelesmatics*, ii. 23; Antiochus, *Treasury* (preserved in Rhetorius, *Astrological Compendium*, Chapter 19); Porphyry, *Introduction to the Tetrabiblos*, Chapt. 33; and Maximus. Ptolemy mentions them in *Tetrabiblos*, i. 15, as being "those parts equidistant from the tropical signs," thus carefully avoiding being too specific, but stating that "the lengths of their own hours are the same." Firmicus, *loc. cit.*, gives a table of *antiscia* based on the Ptolemaic norm of putting the tropic of Cancer at the beginning of the sign. Thus we see that the "seeing signs" are the origin of the *antiscia*, which in turn led to the origin of what we call *parallels* today.
[2] Here and in the following chapters Paul explains the astrological significance of the sign configurations.
[3] Called *prostassonta* (or *keleuonta*) 'commanding' and *akouonta* 'hearing' (= 'hearing and obeying') in Greek. They are mentioned by Ptolemy, *Tetrabiblos*, i. 15, again omitting the names of the sign pairs, and describing them as being "those divisions which are disposed at an equal distance from one or the other of the equinoctial signs" (which agrees with the older pairing) "because they ascend in equal periods of time" (which would demand that they be equidistant from 0 Cancer or Capricorn). This looks like a deliberate effort to give a definition that could be read either way. Manilius, *Astronomica*, 2.485-519, agrees with Paul, as do Antiochus, *Treasury* (preserved in Rhetorius, *Astrological Compendium*,

signs that obey each other correspond to a group of runaways and expatriates, and of rumors along with reports, with the Moon moving in her passage towards the [star] of Mercury or the benefic stars, either in a nativity or in some horary or electional figure of those things being investigated in this regard.

Commanding and Obeying

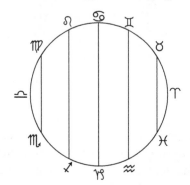

10. *THE TRINE, SEXTILE, SQUARE, AND OPPOSITION ASPECTS.*

Since the whole of the zodiacal circle is composed of 360 degrees; the side[1] of the trine is composed of 5 signs[2] or 120 degrees,[3] for, tripling the 120 degrees, they amount to precisely the 360 degrees of the zodiacal circle.

Chapter 19); Porphyry, *Introduction to the Tetrabiblos*, Chapter 31; Hephaestio, *Apotelesmatics*, ii. 23 (but at i. 9 he repeats the essence of Ptolemy's definition); and Maximus.

[1] Here and subsequently in this chapter Paul uses the term 'side' where we would say 'aspect'. I have retained the literal translation in the first two paragraphs, but thereafter I have translated the Greek term as 'aspect'.

[2] The ancients counted both ends of a sequence, contrary to our practice of only counting one end, so from their point of view Leo is 5 signs from Aries, not 4 signs as we would count it.

[3] Here Paul uses two different systems of specifying the length of the side of a geometrical figure inscribed within a circle: (1) the commonplace method of counting both ends of a sequence of discrete units; and (2) the technical method of counting the number of measurement units (here, degrees) that would fit between two points. This mixing of these two modes

Figures

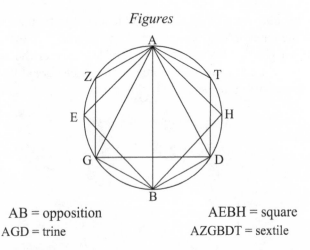

AB = opposition   AEBH = square

AGD = trine   AZGBDT = sextile

The side of the sextile is composed of 3 signs or 60 degrees, for also, multiplying the 60 degrees by 6, they amount to precisely the 360 degrees of the zodiacal circle. And the side of the square is composed of 4 signs or 90 degrees, for, multiplying the 90 degrees by 4, they amount to precisely the 360 degrees of the zodiacal circle; while the composition of the aspect of the opposition is of 7 signs [or] 180 degrees, which being doubled amount to precisely the 360 degrees of the zodiacal circle. And the aspect of the trine is harmonious and harmless, but the square is inharmonious and uneven with regard to the outcome of astrological influences. And the sextile, whenever it is found in the signs that hear each other or see each other, has the power of the trine, [but] the three-sign[1] sextile in the other signs [has only] half[6.17] [the power]. While the

_____

of measurement evidently goes back to one of the early astrological treatises, as it is found in Manilius, Julius Firmicus, and Paul. By contrast, only the second or technical method is used by Geminus, Ptolemy, and Hephaestio of Thebes, which is to be expected, since Geminus and Ptolemy were astronomers and Hephaestio follows Ptolemy very closely.

[1]The addition of the epithet 'three-sign' here is mere verbal ornament, since from the ancients' point of view all sextiles consist of three signs. Note that by restricting the full-powered sextile aspect to pairs of signs that either see or hear each other Paul has reduced the possible number of such sextiles from 12 to only 4, viz. Gemini and Leo, Virgo and Scorpio,

18

aspect of the opposition happens to be discordant and disputed and irregular, yet when the stars are configured together in one and the same sign,[1] their joint presence must be considered harmonious and effective for each of their astrological influences, being equal in power to the trine aspect; but those signs which are separated by other than these intervals are termed *averted* and *inconjunct*.

11. *SIGNS THAT ARE INCONJUNCT WITH EACH OTHER.*

The placement of the signs that are *inconjunct* with each other has its interval from the numbers two and six and eight and twelve,[2] but the signs that have taken [one of] these numbers for this particular interval are also said to be *averted from each other*. And so, when the stars are found in these signs, they are rendered inharmonious; and sometimes they prognosticate enmities and factions, and at other times separations and estrangements of such a kind [as are] experienced in all cases, either in the case of parents and children, or in the case of brothers, or in the case of man and wife, or in the case of companionship, or in the case of slaves and masters, and in the case of all similar associations.

Sagittarius and Aquarius, and Pisces and Taurus. Firmicus, *Mathesis* ii. 22, is more generous. He only downgrades those sextiles that have fixed signs in between: "But those sextiles are more powerful that have cardinal or common signs in the middle, while those that are divided by fixed signs are ineffective."

[1] He means when they are in *conjunction* in the same sign. Since the conjunction is a *position*, it was not considered to be an *aspect* by the ancient astrologers, although they treated it like one.

[2] Counting from one sign to its equal-rising sign in the clockwise direction (and counting both end signs as the ancients were accustomed to do). Thus, Aries to Pisces is 2 signs, Gemini to Capricorn is 6, Cancer to Sagittarius is 8, and Virgo to Libra is 12. Taurus to Aquarius and Leo to Scorpio are omitted because they are in square to each other and consequently not averted. The degree intervals of these combinations are 30 degrees and 150 degrees measured either to the right or the left. By modern astrologers they are reckoned among the "minor aspects" and are called *semi-sextile* and *quincunx* respectively.

12. *[SIGNS] THAT SYMPATHIZE WITH EACH OTHER THOUGH AVERTED.*

Homozones

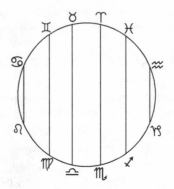

Equal-rising

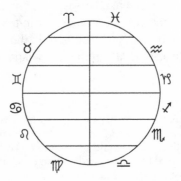

The averted twelfths [of the zodiac] and the [ones that] are un-sympathetic to each other because of *homozone* and rising in the same times do sympathize. But *homozones* are whenever the signs belong to the same star, and *equal-rising* [are] those rising from the invisible into the visible in the same [number of] hours.[1] But those of the *homozone* signs have disagreement through the matter

---

[1]These signs are those that are in what modern astrologers call the *con-tra-antiscion* relationship.

of the *inconjunct* [signs] in this way: Aries [is] against Scorpio, Scorpio against Aries; Taurus against Libra and Libra against Taurus; Capricorn against Aquarius and Aquarius against Capricorn. Of the equal-rising signs the order is this: Aries against Pisces and Gemini against Capricorn and Cancer against Sagittarius and Virgo against Libra, because in fact they are 2 and 6 and 8 and 12 signs from each other. But the ones adjoining each other also have sympathy for each other just as though they were placed next to each other in partnership. But the signs that happen to be [separated] by 6 or 8 or 12[1] have a power just like the opposition aspect, [and] there is greater power in the averted *homozones* and equal-rising [signs] that are on the right[S.18] in this arrangement; for example, in the case of the *homozones* that are averted, Taurus will have more power than Libra and Aries more than Scorpio. In the same way too, in the case of the equal-rising signs, Cancer will be judged to have greater power than Sagittarius and Capricorn will have greater power than Gemini. But the equal-rising signs that are adjacent to each other will similarly have equal power with each other as was said, [when they are] arranged just as in the case of those that are jointly *homozones* or in aspect.

13. *SIGNS THAT ARE IN ASPECT, AND HOMOZONE AND EQUAL-RISING [SIGNS].*

The rest of the *homozone* signs, which are in square to each other, will have double the power of the *homozones* that are arranged in aversion to each other. This is Sagittarius as compared to Pisces and Gemini as compared to Virgo, just as though they were arranged on the right and prepollent. But in the case of the equal-rising and in-aspect [signs], Leo will have greater power as compared to Scorpio and Aquarius as compared to Taurus. For the signs of the *homozone* that are adjacent to each other will have equal power, just as if they had chanced to be in aspect.

---

[1]MS **Z** omits 12, perhaps rightly, since 2 and 12 resemble the conjunction, while 6 and 8 have analogy with the opposition.

14. *THE PHASES THAT THE FIVE STARS MAKE WITH THE SUN.*

The revolving[S.19] stars[1] [S.20] make phases with regard to the Sun —now the morning[S.21] risings and the evening settings,[S.22] now the evening risings and the morning settings of their course, moving into their first and second stations, from which also they first become retrograde and *acronychal*,[2] [and] at other times they are perceived to be direct. And when the stars chance to be in their morning risings, they must be considered to be effective and active[S.23] from [the time of] youth with regard to their own proper significations. And in their evening risings, and with the passage of time, they are effective in their own proper significations. But when they are making their morning or evening disappearance[3] or else retracing their path or when they are cadent, their influences are useless and unfavorable for action and insignificant.

And the stars become morning risers whenever they are distant from the Sun by 15 degrees in the preceding degrees or also in the preceding signs until they are found making their movement up to the dexter trine[S.24] of it; but evening [stars] whenever they are in the following degrees or also in the following signs [and] are distant from the Sun the previously mentioned 15 degrees, until they are found up to the sinister trine[S.25] of it. And when they have their distance to the Sun within the previously mentioned 15 degrees, [and] they are in the degrees rising before the Sun, they make their morning setting, but in the [degrees] rising after [it], an evening [setting].

They become conjunct whenever they happen to be in the same degree as the Sun in the same sign, not being distant from it by

---

[1]The five planets.
[2]*Acronychal* means 'rising as the Sun sets'. In modern astrological terminology, 'opposite the Sun'. And in modern astronomical terminology, simply 'in opposition'.
[3]Presumably, when they are within 9 degrees of the Sun as mentioned below.

more than approximately 59 minutes. Furthermore, the stars become weak and ineffective for action in their own proper significations, whenever one of them is distant from the Sun within 9 degrees [or less], being either in the morning setting or in the evening [setting].

In order to understand the aforesaid readily, we shall employ an example. Let the Sun be in the 17th degree of Pisces, the star of Jupiter in the 2nd degree of the same sign, and Saturn in the 26th degree of Pisces.[1] Then we say the star of Jupiter is *morning rising*, because in the 15 degrees preceding the Sun it is [so] called; but the [star] of Saturn is *evening setting*, because in the degrees following it was not separated from the Sun by the previously mentioned 15 degrees.

In order to make quite plain what was said, the degrees preceding the Sun and the signs preceding it up to the aspect of the trine in the degrees that rise before and on the right side of the Sun are called *matutine*; but the following degrees and the following signs up to the aspect of the trine of the Sun in the degrees that rise after and on the left side of the Sun have the *vespertine* appearance.

And those [stars] that are with the Sun become *doryphories*[S.26] in the degrees preceding the Sun and the signs preceding it up to the aspect of the trine.[2] But those that happen to be with the Moon in the degrees following it up to the next sign [become its doryphories].

But then the doryphories of the stars that are with the Sun are said to be effective and stronger whenever they are found to be eastern risers in the same sign with the Sun in advantageous places[S.27] of the nativity, when they are *in sect*[3] or *dispositors*[4] of

---

[1]These positions are probably arbitrary, selected for illustration only; however, they correspond approximately to 10 March 172.
[2]This is a definition of the term *doryphory*.
[3]That is, when they are diurnal stars by day or nocturnal stars by night.
[4]A planet that rules the sign that another planet is in is said to be its *dis-*

the Sun[S.28]. But in the case of the Moon, the same placement [of the stars] must also be considered to be more active and more effective.

15. *STATIONS.*

The stations of the stars are different and not the same.[1] When the [stars] of Saturn and of Jupiter and of Mars are distant from the Sun by 120 degrees more or less[2] and appear in right trine to it, they make their first station; and moving more slowly, they turn around at the same degree, until, retracing their path, they become[S.29] retrograde—turning from the first of these stations into retrograding, but turning into direct motion from the second.

And generally[S.30] the three previously mentioned stars become retrograde whenever they are 6 or 7 or 8 signs distant from the Sun. And appearing in opposition to it in 180 degrees, which is 7 signs,[3] from the solar ray, they have[S.31] their *acronychal* phase, and going back further they are retrograde, and they appear greater in their circumference,[4] since they are getting the radiant light from the ray of the Sun.

---

positor. Here we have a special case.

[1] That is, the stations of the outer planets (Mars, Jupiter, and Saturn) are different from those of the inner planets (Mercury and Venus).

[2] The figure of 120 degrees is mentioned by several of the Greek astrologers and by Pliny. It is only an approximation to the truth, and Paul indicates this by adding the phrase "more or less" to it. Since Mars is closest to the earth and has the second most eccentric orbit, its elongation from the Sun at the stationary points shows the greatest variation, sometimes being as much as 150 degrees. However, since Pliny mentions 120 degrees, the figure is pre-Ptolemaic and probably refers to the *Eternal Tables*, which were perhaps constructed on a different mathematical model from Ptolemy's epicyclic theory.

[3] Remember that Paul's "6, 7, or 8" signs is what we would call "5, 6, or 7 signs."

[4] This seems to refer to the fact that the outer planets, especially Mars, are noticeably brighter at opposition and hence appear to be "larger in size." (And in fact they do have a larger semi-diameter as seen in a telescope.)

But the second station of the previously mentioned stars occurs whenever they are distant 120 degrees more or less in the following direction[1] of the ray of the Sun, when the stars are in left trine to the Sun, and, beginning to move forward in this aspect, they make their motion swifter [and] they become direct; whence properly, these [positions] were styled "stations." The first then of the stationary positions of the stars and their [subsequent] going back while retrograding was styled "static retrograde." But the second of the stationary positions and the turning direct in swifter motion was styled "static direct."

They are said [to be] *acronychal*, since being in opposition to the Sun, they rise after its setting. But only the star of Mars moves anomalously[S.32] whenever it is about to become stationary. And it makes its first *anomaly* when, as a morning riser, it is distant from the Sun by 82 degrees moving into its first station, but the second [anomaly] when, as an evening riser, it appears separated from the Sun by the same 82 degrees, moving direct from its second station. These [positions] were styled *anomalies* [S.33] because the star makes its motion anomalously when posited in these configurations.[2] But this star always makes either its first or second anomaly

---

[1]Remember that the terms "following" and "preceding" usually refer to the direction of the diurnal motion. Hence, a star that is "following" the Sun rises after it. But since the numbering of the signs of the zodiac is in the opposite direction to the diurnal motion, a star that is "following the Sun" is more advanced in the zodiac. For example, if the Sun is in Taurus and Mars is in Gemini, then the Sun will rise first and Mars will *follow* it by rising after the Sun. Conversely, if Mars is in Pisces, then it would *precede* the Sun from Paul's point of view.

[2]The purpose of the "82 degree anomalies" is uncertain. O. Neugebauer, *A History of Ancient Mathematical Astronomy* (New York Heidelberg Berlin: Springer-Verlag, 1975), vol. ii, p. 792, discusses these "anomalies" and cites Pliny, NH, II. 60, Porphyry, *Introduction to the Tetrabiblos*, Chapt. 2, as well as this chapter of Paul, and Heliodorus's *Commentary on Paul*. Neugebauer thinks these 82 degree points are elongations from the Sun within which the planet is retrograde, and that they were useful as an aid to computing the position of the planet during the period of retrogradation. It seems likely that since these "anomalies" are mentioned by Pliny, they must be related to some pre-Ptolemaic

whenever[S.34] it beholds the Sun. . . .[1]

{....it devastates the paternal substance and becomes destructive to the father himself. But for these also it becomes the cause of injuries or sicknesses, especially of the eyes, or of madness. But the sicknesses are also affecting the father or affecting the nativity itself. For if the Sun is aided by benefics, for example by Jupiter or the Moon, being aspected by them or angular or in benefic [houses], then the father is not harmed, [and] you will examine the harm [as] affecting the nativity, affecting the sight and the authoritative [part of the mind], for the Sun is lord of these. And if the Sun is afflicted but the ASC is aided, the father is destroyed, for indeed the Sun has analogy with the father, [but] the ASC with the native. And when the Moon is afflicted, it does the same thing to the mother....}[2]

When the [stars] of Venus and Mercury are in the stations of their course, they have their change [of direction] differently, for the first station in the case of these two stars occurs in different degrees, and [the star of Venus] is stationary whenever it is 48 degrees distant[1] from the Sun in the following direction; for then it

---

planetary tables that were commonly used by astrologers, perhaps the so-called *Eternal Tables*. Hence, they were an ephemeris computing aid, not points of astrological significance.

[1]The distance is missing along with the rest of the sentence, and the following passage enclosed in braces does not belong here.

[2]The former part of this astrological interpolation is found in MS **Y** and the MSS of the Beta and Gamma families, but the latter part of the passage, beginning with the words "For if the Sun...", is found only in MS **Y**. Interestingly enough, the *Summary*, which is also contained in MS **Y**, does not mention anything purely astrological in Chapter 15. We are thus faced with two possibilities: either the author of the *Summary* overlooked the astrological portion of Chapter 15, or else it was not present in his exemplar. Also, the Scholia take no note of it. I am inclined to think that it was accidentally incorporated into the text of the subarchetype. Whether it is a stray part of Paul's text or derives from some other source I do not venture to guess at this point.

[1]Actually, only about 28°, although the maximum elongation is about 48°. As Neugebauer points out (HAMA, p. 804), Paul has confused the

begins to go back and to be retrograde, making its motion slower, until, conjoining the Sun, it comes into its morning rising and is distant from the Sun the same 48 degrees, and [then] it will make its second station.

But the star of Mercury makes its first station whenever it is 22 degrees distant[1] from the Sun in the following sign; and then similarly it begins to go back, making its motion slower, until, after conjoining the Sun, it comes to its morning rising and is distant from the Sun the same 22 degrees, and [then] it will make its second station. The [star] of Venus does not separate from the Sun more than two signs, and the [star] of Mercury separates only one sign. The *Handy Tables*[S.35] of Claudius Ptolemy will provide accuracy for these [stars].

---

maximum elongations with the first and second stations (SR_x and SD) stations. They are not the same. When Venus is moving direct, its daily motion in longitude is usually greater than the Sun's daily motion. But when it nears its first station, it begins to slow down; and when its daily motion decreases until it becomes equal to the Sun's daily motion, it reaches its maximum elongation. Thereafter, its daily motion continues to decrease until it reaches 0, at which time it turns retrograde. About 20 days later it conjoins the Sun; and after another 22 days or so it turns direct. But once it begins to move forward it is about 29° behind the Sun in the zodiac, and its daily motion must increase from 0 to that of the Sun before it reaches its maximum elongation from the Sun. This requires about 50 days.

[1] Again Paul has confused the times of maximum elongation with the stations. The result is similar to that described in the preceding footnote. However, the maximum elongation of Mercury is not 22°, but it ranges from 18° to 28° (due to Mercury's eccentric orbit). Neugebauer (*loc. cit.*) notes that Paul's figures for Venus and Mercury, 48° and 22° respectively also appear in the Michigan Astrological Papyrus (*P. Mich. 149*, Sect. x) which is assigned to the second century, so they evidently reflect some non-Ptolemaic planetary theory, perhaps that of the *Eternal Tables*. (Ptolemy's figures are 48° and 28°.)

16. *THE CONFIGURATIONS THAT THE MOON*
MAKES WITH THE SUN.

The configurations of the Moon, which are called *phases*,[S.36] are these[1]: *conjunction*,[2] *coming forth*, *rising*, *crescent*,[3] *half*,[4] *gibbous*, *full Moon*, *gibbous* again, and *second half*, and *crescent*. But some also mention an 11th phase, calling it *nearly bright* or *nearly full*. And the *conjunction* is when the Moon chances to be in the same degree with the Sun; *coming forth*, when it goes one degree past the Sun; *rising*, when it passes 15 degrees; *first crescent* appears when the Moon, on the following side,[5] of the Sun, is separated from it by 60 degrees, [and] is in sextile aspect; *first half*[6] is when the Moon, on the following side of the Sun, is separated from it by 90 degrees, [and] is in square aspect.

First gibbous is when the Moon, on the following side of the Sun, is separated from it by 120 degrees, [and] is placed in trine aspect to it; *nearly full*, when it chances to be 6 signs or 150 degrees on the following side of the Sun, not yet making the opposition; *full Moon* is when, on the following side of the Sun, the Moon is distant from it by 180 degrees, [and] is placed in the opposition position, which is called "the full Moon conjunction."

Waning is when the Moon passes the solar opposition by one degree; [and] it is [still] called waning up to 60 degrees. *Second gibbous* is when, on the side behind[7] the Sun, it is separated from it

---

[1]Reading *esti tade* 'are these' with MSS **Zβγ** rather than *eisin deka* 'are ten' with MSS **LY**. There are actually 7 phases, as Vettius Valens says in *Anthology* ii. 36.
[2]We would say "new Moon."
[3]Literally, 'moon-shaped'.
[4]It is called *half* because of its appearance. We would say it is at its *quarter* because it assumes that appearance at the first and third quarters of the lunar month.
[5]That is, 'following' in the diurnal motion. He refers to the waxing phase of the Moon, when it is passing from new to full.
[6]From the Moon's actual appearance. We call this phase the 'first quarter' because it marks the end of the first quarter of the lunar month.
[7]That is, 'behind' in the zodiac. A curious choice of terms, since he calls

by 120 degrees, [and] is placed in trine aspect. *Second half*[1] is when again the Moon, from that same side of the Sun, is distant from it by 90 degrees, [and] is in square aspect. *Second crescent* is when, from the side behind the Sun, it is distant from it by 60 degrees, [and is] in the sextile aspect.

And fittingly, these terms were coined to suit the variation in configurations. For the *conjunction* was so called from the joining together of the Moon with the Sun. *Coming forth* was so called from the going out of the Moon from the Sun, when, having passed by the first degree itself, it begins to appear in the cosmos, not as [it does] to us.[2] *Rising*, when, passing by 15 degrees, it appears assuming the form of a thin streak of light. *Crescent* was so called since it appears assuming that same form, for the Moon itself is crescent-shaped,[3] since it also makes the rising (phase) lunar.

Half was so called because when it grows to half its full amount of light, it appears to be divided in two. *Gibbous* was so called, since from both sides the look of the light of it appears to be humped. N*early full* was so called when it appeared from the sixth sign,[S.37] and *full Moon* because it was filled up with light from the rays of the Sun, appearing to the opposite of it, whenever it has filled up the brightness of its light, then it also appears similar to a circular shape, having become the *full Moon. Waning* was so

---

the other side 'following' and things that *follow* are usually also *behind*. But *following* and *preceding* usually refer to directions in the diurnal motion, i.e. to positions that are to the left (sinister) or to the right (dexter) of the point in question.

[1] We would say 'third quarter' or 'last quarter', again referring to the *time* of the lunar month rather than to the actual *appearance* of the Moon in the sky.

[2] That is, it has already passed the Sun in the sky, but we cannot yet see it because it is still too close to the Sun.

[3] It is difficult here to imitate the Greek in the translation. The word normally used for 'moon' is *Selênê*, but there is another word *mênê* that also means 'moon', and it is this latter word that forms part of the compound *mênoeidês* 'moon-shaped', which I have translated as 'crescent'. Literally, '"Moon-shaped" was so called since it appears assuming that same form, for Selene herself is the Moon'. . . .

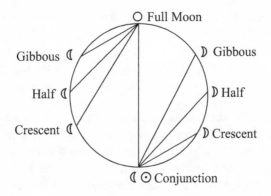

O Full Moon
Gibbous ☾   ☽ Gibbous
Half ☾   ☽ Half
Crescent ☾   ☽ Crescent
☾ ☉ Conjunction

called because having passed by the rays of the opposition, from then on there is waning and lessening of its light.

17. *THE SEPARATIONS AND APPLICATIONS THAT THE MOON MAKES WITH THE REVOLVING STARS.*

Since the topic of application and separation is a varied one, it is necessary to provide an explanation of it. And it is this: with whatever star the Moon chances to be, if it has more degrees in the same sign, it has made its separation from it; but if the one of the stars that is with the Moon in the same sign has more degrees of the sign, that same one receives its application. But in the same manner also, if the stars are found in the sign following the Moon or in the one preceding, being within a space of 30 degrees, they are [also] included in the topic of separation and application.

By way of illustration, with the Moon in the 20th degree of Sagittarius, the [star] of Mars in the 20th degree of Scorpio, and the [star] of Venus in the 20th degree of Capricorn, we say the separation of the Moon from the [star] of Mars has occurred, and the application to the star of Venus has been made.[1] And so too when the

---

[1]This is an illustration of the 30 degree rule that applies to an extended bodily separation and application. It does not refer to the 30-degree as-

stars are in the same sign with the Moon, one must treat either the separations or the applications according to their presence. Let us say the Moon is in the 10th degree of Taurus, the [star] of Mercury in the 9th degree, and the [star] of Jupiter in the 11th degree. We say then that the Moon has made a separation from the [star] of Mercury and an application to the star of Jupiter.[1]

But the condition of separation and application is always extremely effective for the illustration of astrological influences when it is in effect [first] from the first [degree] up to three degrees,[S.38] and second [within] the distance from the first degree having the number[2] up to the 7th degree of the previously mentioned pattern of degrees, and third from the first degree up to the 15th, and fourth it is in effect for the condition of separation and application from the first degree up to the 30th. From the latter [three] distances, in the case of either separation or application, it has its effect in the later times [of life] and not from youth; I mean, it makes the final outcome of those things that will be either good or bad [to occur] from middle age [on] or even in old age.[3]

We shall also employ another instructive example for more complete knowledge of the topic of separation and application. Let us say, the Moon [is] in the 13th degree of Libra, and the [star] of Mars in the 6th degree, [and] the [star] of Jupiter is in the 20th degree of the same sign; [then] the Moon has separated from [star] of Mars and applied to the [star] of Jupiter within the space of seven degrees.

---

pect (the semisextile), which was unknown to the ancients. In modern terms, it amounts to allowing a 30-degree orb to the conjunction.
[1]This entire paragraph is omitted by MS **Y** and the MSS of the β family.
[2]Namely the degree number where the conjunction is exact.
[3]This means that the time of life in which the separation or application will manifest itself is a function of its distance from the faster moving body (here, the Moon). If the distance is less than 3 degrees, it will act in youth; if the distance is between 3 and 7 degrees, it will act in the prime of life; if it is between 7 and 15 degrees, it will act in the later years; and if it is between 15 and 30 degrees, it will act in old age.

While discussing the varieties of the [Moon's] separation from and application to the stars, both by aspects and by wind,[1] either by trine, or by sextile, or by square or opposition, [we may say that] there is an application by trine aspect within 120 to 117 degrees, or by sextile within 60 to 57 degrees, or by square within 90 to 87 degrees, or by opposition within 180 to 177, with the stars being in either right or left aspect to the Moon..

For example, in the case of the trine aspect, let it be given [that] the Moon is in the 15th degree of Aries and Jupiter in the 18th to the 15th degree of Sagittarius; we say [that] an application of the Moon to the [star] of Jupiter has been made by right trine. And similarly too in the case of the remaining aspects when the Moon is aspecting the stars partilely, one must assume that the separation or application of the Moon to the stars arising from the motion[S.39] of the wind has the same action when the Moon goes up and down that same wind in the course of the revolving stars, [as it does] when [it goes up and down] another [wind].[2]

---

[1] The Greek text has *kai kata skhêmata kai kata anemon* 'both by aspect and by wind', where 'by wind' refers to the direction (i.e. North or South) of the latitude of the Moon or the star it is configured with. The remainder of the paragraph seems to say that it doesn't matter whether the Moon and the star have the same direction of latitude or not – the effect is the same in either case, which is what Ptolemy says in the latter part of *Tetrabiblos*, i. 24. However, in the earlier part of that chapter, Ptolemy says that it does make a difference in the case of separations and applications by body, and Paul does not mention that. Hence, it seems pointless to have mentioned the direction of the latitudes at all. Curiously enough, Heliodorus's *Commentary on Paul*, Chapter 16, goes on for four pages explaining separations and applications 'by aspect' and 'by body', but never says a word about 'by wind'. This inclines me to think that the text Heliodorus had in front of him did not contain the latter part of the paragraph in which the wind is mentioned, since it is so obscurely worded that Heliodorus could scarcely have resisted the temptation to try to explain it.

[2] This seems to say that the astrological indications are the same, whether or not the two bodies have the same direction of latitude. But Ptolemy thought that while this was true in the case of aspects, it was not true for conjunctions. See Scholium 39, where the scholiast attempts to clarify Paul's statement.

Without the matter of separation and application, neither longevity, nor brevity of life, nor sickness, nor injury, nor wealth, nor misfortune, nor fame, nor obscurity, nor manliness, nor weakness is established in the nativity.[1] [S.40]

18. *FOREKNOWLEDGE OF THE WINDS.*[S.41]

It is possible to know the winds that are about to blow from the separations and applications of the Moon [and] from the triplicities. For if the Moon has an application by trine or a separation by trine with some star in the first triplicity Aries-Leo-Sagittarius, [the wind] will be *Apeliotes* (the East Wind); in the second triplicity Taurus-Virgo-Capricorn, *Notos* (the South Wind); in the third triplicity Gemini-Libra-Aquarius, the wind becomes westerly[2]; and in the fourth triplicity Cancer-Scorpio-Pisces, *Borras* (the North Wind). And whether [it will be] stormy or calm may be known from the nature of the star.

19. *THE KNOWLEDGE OF HOW MANY ARE THE DAYS OF THE GODS.*[S.42]

For the year you are seeking, add a fourth[S.43] of the time from Diocletian to 2 in every case, and divide the resulting number by 7; and say [that] those that remain are the *Days of the Gods*.[3]

---

[1] That is, the applications and separations of the Moon establish the general pattern for these facets of human life—a pattern that would not exist without their special influences.

[2] Its Greek name is *Lips*.

[3] The formula is very simple: Days of the Gods = (Y + INT(Y/4) + 2) MOD 7, where Y is the year number, INT(Y/4) is the integer number of 4's contained in Y, 2 is a constant, and "MOD 7" means to find the integer remainder from dividing the summation within the parentheses by 7. To use Paul's example of the Year 94 Diocletian, the Days of the Gods = (94 + INT(94/4) + 2) MOD 7 = (94 + 23 + 2) MOD 7 = 119 MOD 7 = 0. But since the ancients did not use 0 as a number, we add 7 and say that the Days of the Gods are 7. This number is good for the entire year 94 Diocletian. It is 3 less than the weekday number of the 1st day of the year (1 Thoth). The rationale behind the calculation is this: a common year

For example, I seek out the measure of the 94th year of Diocletian thus[1]: how many are the Days of the Gods. I found a fourth[S.44] of these [years] to be 23; then [adding] to these the previously mentioned "2 in-every-case," and combining [their sum] with the 94, the result is 119. Divide [this] by 7: 7 times 10 [is] 70, 7 times 6 [is] 42, [with] 7 remaining.[2] We say [that] these are the Days of the Gods.[3]

But if the number is found full and nothing is left over, we call it "6th day."[4]

20. *THE KNOWLEDGE OF EACH DAY: TO WHICH OF THE GODS IT BELONGS.*

Multiplying by 2 the months from Thoth, up to the one you are seeking,[5] you add to the number resulting from the doubling, the Days of the Gods that have been found[S.45] for that time; and to the combined number you also add the [day] number of the month; and, dividing the resulting number by 7, cast the remainder from

---

consists of 365 days, which is 52,1 weeks (52 weeks plus 1 day), and a leap year consists of 366 days, which is 52,2 weeks. As good luck would have it, the first leap year in this era fell in Year 3, so for Year 3 the formula yields Days of the Gods = (3 + 0 + 2) MOD 7 = 5, and for Year 4 Days of the Gods = (4 +1 +2) MOD 7 = 0, which we call 7. Thus, New Year's Day of 4 Diocletian was 2 days later in the week than New Year's Day of 3 Diocletian, which is correct because 3 Diocletian was a leap year.

[1]This year began on 29 August 377.

[2]Note how Paul divides 119 by 7: he successively removes easy multiples of 7 until the remainder is 7 or less.

[3]By "days of the gods" Paul means "days of the week." The purpose of this calculation is to determine a number that is 3 less than the number of the day of the week on which 1 Thoth falls for the year of Diocletian in question. See the Commentary for a more detailed explanation of the theory. In the present example, notice that in dividing the 119 days by 7, Paul has avoided the result 17,0 by taking it as 16,7.

[4]This is at variance with the example just given and is also wrong. Either it should read "7th day" or the whole sentence should be deleted as an incorrect interpolation.

[5]Paul means to multiply the month number itself by 2.

the day of the Sun (Sunday) in the order of the [days of the] week, giving to each of the stars one day, and you will find which of the stars it is whose day you are seeking.[1]

For example, we seek out what day it is today, which is 20 Mecheir of the 94th year from Diocletian.[S.46] Since therefore from Thoth up to Mecheir is 6 months,[2] we double these up and they make 12; but for this particular year [the days of the gods] are 7; we add these to the doubled number of the months, and they make 19; to this 19 we add on top the sought for 20th of the month; it makes 39 days. We divide these by 7: 5 times 7 [is] 35, [with] remainder 4. We cast the 4 from the day of the Sun, and we compute [them] following in the order of the [days of the] week, reckoning the first [day] to the Sun, and giving the second to the Moon, assigning the third to Mars, and the fourth to Mercury. Then it is the yielded day of Mercury according to the preceding method.[3]

---

[1]The formula is this: $(2 M + D + G)$ MOD 7, where M is the month number, D is the day of the month number, G is the Days of the Gods number, and "MOD 7" means to divide the summation in the parentheses by 7 and save the remainder, which is the weekday number. Paul calls Sunday the 1st day of the week. The rationale behind the calculation is this: the Alexandrian calendar consisted of 12 months of 30 days each, followed by 5 additional days in common years and 6 additional days in leap years. (For the purposes of this calculation, the 5 or 6 days could be considered to be a 13th month.) A month of 30 days is 4,2 weeks (4 weeks + 2 days), so the 1st of each month is 2 days later in the week than the 1st day of the preceding month. Hence, to take this 2-day advance into account, you simply double the month number. (We would double M-1, but the extra 2 days we get by doubling M is allowed for in the constant 2 that is used to find the Days of the Gods.) Then we add the number of the day of the month, and finally we cast out multiples of 7. The end result is the day of the week determined from the Alexandrian date with the year from Diocletian. Scholium 46 contains a medieval scholiast's attempt to explain the procedure.
[2]Mecheir is the 6th month of the Egyptian calendar; hence, counting both ends as usual, Mecheir is 6 months from the first month Thoth.
[3]In the preceding chapter Paul calculated the "Days of the Gods," which is a number good for the whole year (rather like the Dominical Letter of our calendar). In this chapter he adds the "Days of the Gods" number to numbers depending on the month number and the day number. Dividing the sum by 7 he gets the remainder 4, which is the day of the week. Count-

21. THE DAY RULER AND THE HOUR RULER.

It will be necessary to look at the day-ruler[1] and the hour-ruler[2] in each nativity and for every day arising from the placement of the stars in the sphere following the serial order of the *heptazone*. For by means of these it is possible to understand the sudden occurrences in agreements and in promises and in favors and benefits; the inquiry itself [is] useful in [the matter of the] success of alliance with those who are in authority or with persons in power with regard to penalties or accusations and imprisonment and anguish, slanders and false accusations, and entanglements, and losses, and thefts, and making wills; and in sailing and trade and traveling, we will [also] discover combat and uproars and decumbitures and things similar to these. And it is useful to physicians for examination, both in procedures involving the sick and in those of surgery or healing, [and] for making an infallible election for the previously mentioned matters.

But the order of the *heptazone* is this: the star of Saturn was allotted the first and highest zone, being very cold and lying in the frost. And the [star] of Jupiter rules the second, temperate and nourishing, and life-producing. And the [star] of Mars was allotted the third and fiery zone [that] is destructive. And the Sun was as-

---

ing this off, beginning with Sunday, he gets Wednesday for his date 20 Mecheir 94 Diocletian. This is equivalent to 14 February 378 A.D. and serves to date the composition of the book.

[1] From the Greek *poleuôn* 'revolving', perhaps in reference to the rotation of the earth during a 24-hour period. It is the planet which presides over the whole day and gives its name to it, as the Sun presides over Sunday.

[2] From the Greek *diepôn* 'managing'. Liddell & Scott say the verb *diepô* means 'to manage' and they add "esp. as a deputy or substitute," which is exactly how it is used here. It is the planet which rules a single hour of a day (or night) as a sub-ruler under the day-ruler. In modern astrology it is called "the ruler of the planetary hour." Note that the "hours of the day" are counted from sunrise, and the "hours of the night" are counted from sunset. These are called "seasonal hours" because their length (in mean hours and minutes) varies with the seasons, the "hours of the day" being longer in summer and shorter in winter, and the "hours of the night" the reverse.

signed the fourth and middle zone of the Ether, being fiery and life-producing. Venus, being allotted the fifth and pleasant zone, became the cause of conception and offspring. The star of Mercury was allotted the sixth and common zone, which is moist. But the the most powerful Moon received the seventh, since it is also a zone that is moist and nearer the earth, and accepting the separations of the stars, holding the zones higher than hers, she causes the increase and decrease of all things, indicating by means of her own appearance the life of men in [all] its unevenness.

But the method of the day-ruler and the hour-ruler, either for each day or for a nativity, is this: Let it be the day of Saturn (Saturday). This same star becomes lord of the day and rules the whole day. During the first hour, it is [both] day-ruler and hour-ruler; [after which] it hands the second hour over to Jupiter, and we say that Saturn is day-ruler, with Jupiter as hour-ruler. Then it hands the third hour over to Mars, and we say [that] Saturn is day-ruler, with Mars as hour-ruler; the fourth [hour] to the Sun, with Saturn as day-ruler, Venus as hour-ruler; and the fifth to Venus, with Saturn as day-ruler, Venus as hour-ruler; the sixth to Mercury, with Saturn as day-ruler, Mercury as hour-ruler; and the seventh to the Moon, with Saturn as day-ruler, [and] the Moon as hour-ruler.

But during the eighth [hour], Saturn itself again is day-ruler and hour-ruler; and during the ninth [hour], Saturn is day-ruler, with Jupiter as hour-ruler; and during the tenth, Saturn rules the day, with Mars as hour-ruler; and during the eleventh, Saturn rules the day, with the Sun as hour-ruler; and during the twelfth [hour], Saturn rules the day, with Venus as hour-ruler.

And during the first nocturnal hour of the nocturnal sect, Saturn itself is again the day-ruler, with Mercury following along in turn as hour-ruler; and during the second hour, Saturn is the day-ruler, with the Moon as hour-ruler; however, during the third hour Saturn itself again is [both] the day-ruler and the hour-ruler; and so on until the night is completed, and it becomes Sunday.

For then again the Sun is day-ruler and hour-ruler the whole day and also the following night; and more strongly yet it rules the day and personally rules the first hour; but the second [hour] when the Sun is day-ruler, Venus is said to rule; and the third, Mercury; and the fourth, the Moon; and the fifth, Saturn; and the sixth, Jupiter; and the seventh, Mars; with the Sun again ruling the day and the eighth hour; and so on in the same fashion as the sequence has it.

22. *THE DODECATEMORIES.*

The dodecatemory[1] of the stars and of any particular angle or lot must be worked out thus: for the star or angle or lot whose dodecatemory you are seeking, multiply the degrees it has by 13 S.47 and cast the resulting number from it,[2] reckoning 30 degrees to each sign, and wherever the combined number leaves off, say that the dodecatemory of the star or angle or lot you are seeking is

---

[1]Each sign is divided into twelve 2 ½ degree subdivisions which are assigned to the signs of the zodiac in their usual order, beginning with the sign itself. For example, the first dodecatemory of Aries is Aries, the second is Taurus, the third is Gemini, etc.; the first dodecatemory of Taurus is Taurus, the second is Gemini, the third is Cancer, etc. But since the usual question in the astrologer's mind was, "Which of the dodecatemories is a particular planet or other point in the zodiac in?," it became customary to use the phrase "the dodecatemory of the star." Hence, the phrase "Jupiter's dodecatemory is Leo" means that Jupiter is in a dodecatemory that is ruled by the sign Leo. The earliest known Greek astrologer to mention the dodecatemories is Balbillus (first century), and they are mentioned in two papyrus horoscopes. Pingree (*The Yavanajâtaka of Sphujidhvaja*, vol. 2, p. 210) cites two papers by Neugebauer and Sachs that trace the ultimate origin of the dodecatemories (of the signs) to Babylonian astrology.

[2]By 'it', Paul seems to refer to the starting position, but the product is actually cast from the beginning of the sign containing the starting position. Perhaps he had in mind the fact that one could also multiply the starting degrees by 12 and then add the number of the starting degree to the product. The same thing is accomplished by multiplying by 13, which is a shortcut method. For example, multiply the 11 degrees by 12; it makes 132; then add the original 11 degrees to it; the result is 143, and the dodecatemory will be in 23 Leo as before. But multiplying by 13 is an alternative procedure that is inconsistent with the usual procedure of subtracting multiples of 2 ½ degrees.

there.[1] For example, let us say the [star] of Mercury is in the 11th degree of Aries. Multiplying the 11 by the 13, they become 143; and casting these from the sign in which the star is, giving 30 degrees to each sign, there remain 23. We say the dodecatemory of Mercury is in the 23rd degree of Leo.[2]

The dodecatemory of the benefics produces much when it falls in the sign in which the Sun or the Moon or the star of Mercury is, or on one of the four angles, or on the Lot of Fortune or the Lot of the Daemon or the Lot of Necessity, or on either the preceding conjunction (new Moon) or the full Moon; for by this theory, successful and long-lived and happy men will certainly be signified; just as indeed, if the dodecatemory of the malefic stars falls in the sign in which the Sun, the Moon , or the star of Mercury is, or on one of the four angles, or on the Lot of Fortune or the Lot of the Daemon or the Lot of Necessity, or on the preceding conjunction or the full Moon, it indicates those who are poor and unsuccessful at acquiring property and [generally] unfortunate, as well as ordaining those who are short-lived, or who die violently, or who are sickly or accident prone.

---

[1]This is the second of two methods that the Greek astrologers used to find the dodecatemory of a point in the zodiac. The original method consisted of subtracting multiples of 2 ½ degrees from the longitude of the point until that amount could no longer be subtracted; then, the number of multiples that had been subtracted was counted off from the sign of the point, and the dodecatemory was in the next sign. This could also be accomplished by multiplying the longitude of the point within its sign by 12 and adding the product to the longitude of the beginning of the sign. Paul's method measures the product from the point itself, which is not consistent with the original method of subdividing a sign into twelfths. The original method is followed by Dorotheus, Ptolemy, Antiochus (probably), Porphyry, Firmicus, Hephaestio, and Rhetorius. Interestingly, Rhetorius notes that Paul multiplies by 13, but he says that he has verified by experiment that multiplying by 12 is the correct way.

[2]Here, the proportional position of the planet within the Leo dodecatemory is equated to the 23rd degree of Leo. And in effect this gives the planet two positions within the zodiac: (1) its actual position in 11 Aries; and (2) its derived position in 23 Leo. This is an earlier analogue of the Hindu practice of finding the position of the planets and the ASC in the ninths of the signs.

ANOTHER OF PAUL'S [CHAPTERS].[1]

Multiplying by 13 the degrees of the sign which the star possesses, cast from the sign in which the star is, giving 30 to each sign, and where the number leaves off, say the star's dodecatemory is there, e.g. as in the said example. Let the Moon be in the 13th degree of Aries. Multiply the 13 by 13. They make 169. Of these, I give up to 30 to Aries, to Taurus, to Gemini, to Cancer, and to Leo. There remains 19. And the dodecatemory of the Moon is in Virgo, as also in the first method. But this latter [method] is better than the first by far, because with this latter the dodecatemory of the star can be found in the same sign, and also in the same sign after a circle [has been deducted], in which [the star's] position is.[2]

---

[1]This chapter is only preserved in a single MS (Par. Gr. 2507). It does not appear to be part of Paul's text, but may be a gloss on a scholium of Demophilus (10th century) on Porphyry, *Introduction to the Tetrabiblos*, Chapter 39 (see Bouché-Leclercq, *L'Astrologie Grecque*, p. 302 n.1).
[2]This method is exactly the same as that explained in the preceding section. But it gives a different example and refers to it as if it had been used previously, which it has not. (Porphyry, *op. cit.*, Chapter 39, has an example for the Moon in 13 Aries, but he finds the dodecatemory by successively removing 2 ½ degrees.) Also, it says that this method (multiplying by 13) is better than the other method (presumably, multiplying by 12) when a whole circle is involved. *Cf.* Heliodorus, Chapter 21 (ed. Boer, p. 43,21 ff.) "The *dodecatemorion of the stars...* It is proper to seek what is said to be the dodecatemorion, [from] the position of each star and the multiplication of it by 13, and we mean [that which] the ancients of the Egyptians used to call the dodecatemorion, since they multiplied the number [of degrees] found in the position of each star by 12. However, Paul being later [in time] than "the ancients" and having perceived that the multiplication by 12 never restored [the dodecatemorion] to the same sign where the star is whose dodecatemorion we are seeking—it follows that many times the dodecatemorion of the star falls in the same sign in which the star itself [is posited]." Heliodorus goes on at length, but the problem Paul was trying to deal with was this: If you calculate the dodecatemorion of a point in the 30th degree of Aries by the original method, you get 12 X 30 = 360, and casting that from the beginning of Aries, you get 30 Pisces. Paul thought (wrongly) that you ought to get Aries, so he decided to multiply by 13 instead of 12. By doing this, you get 13 X 30 = 390, and, subtracting 360, you have 30 Aries, which is the sign from which you started and where Paul thought the dodecatemorion

23. *THE SEVEN LOTS ACCORDING TO THE* PANARETOS.[s.48]

The first lot[1] is the Lot of Fortune, which for those who are born by day it will be necessary to count from the solar degree to the lunar degree; and it is necessary to cast the resulting number from the ASC, counting by degrees, giving 30 degrees to each sign, and wherever the resulting number leaves off, say that the Lot of Fortune is there. But for those [who are born] by night, the reverse, i.e. [count] from the lunar degree to the solar. Similarly, it is necessary to cast the number from the degree of the ASC.

The second lot is the Lot of the Daemon, which you will count in diurnal births from the degree of the Moon to the degree of the Sun; and it is necesaary to cast the resulting number from the degree of the ASC, again similarly allotting 30 degrees to each sign, and wherever the number leaves off, there is the Lot of the Daemon. And thus by day, but by night the reverse

---

ought to be. But this cannot be correct because by definition the last dodecatemory of Aries must be Pisces, not Aries. And procedures equivalent to the multiplication by 12 go back ultimately to the Babylonians. See Ulla Koch-Westenholz, *Mesopotamian Astrology* (Copenhagen: Museum Tusculanum Press, 1995), pp. 168-169.

[1]The word 'lot' is a translation of the Greek *klêros*; the corresponding Latin word is *sors*, which means the same thing. Both referred originally to small numbered balls that were selected at random to decide some issue or to allocate something to one or more people. Hence, the word 'lot' acquired the figurative meaning of 'luck' or 'fate' or 'destiny'. In the earliest times the astrological lots were determined on a whole sign basis, so Firmicus, for example, calls them *loci* 'places'. Later, when astrologers began to determine them by degree, the lot was found to lie in a certain *degree*, and the Latin word for degree is *pars* 'part'; hence we speak of the Part of Fortune, and all the numerous lots are called 'parts'. The ones under discussion here are apparently the oldest, since they are attributed to Hermes Trismegistus. They have all fallen out of use with the exception of the first two, the Lot of Fortune and the Lot of the Daemon, which Ptolemy combined into what is called today the Part of Fortune. (By the ancient definition, Ptolemy's Lot of Fortune was the Lot of Fortune by day but the Lot of the Daemon by night.)

The third lot is the Lot of Love, which you will count for those who are born by day from the Lot of the Daemon to the degree of Venus and an equal [number of degrees] from the ASC. But for those [who are born] by night, the reverse.

The fourth lot is the Lot of Necessity, which you will also reckon for those who are born by day from the degree of Mercury to the Lot of Fortune and an equal [number of degrees] from the ASC. But for those [who are born] by night, the reverse.

The fifth lot is the Lot of Boldness, which you will work out from the degree of Mars to the Lot of Fortune for those who are born by day, and an equal [number of degrees] from the ASC. But for those [who are born] by night, the reverse.

The sixth lot is the Lot of Victory, which you will count for those who are born by day from the Lot of the Daemon to the degree of Jupiter, and an equal [number of degrees] from the ASC. But for those [who are born] by night, the reverse.

The seventh lot is the Lot of Retribution, which you will count in diurnal births from Saturn to the Lot of Fortune, and an equal [number of degrees] from the ASC. But by night, the reverse.

As is reasonable, the lots have the same origin, since the Moon naturally becomes Fortune, the Sun Daemon, Venus Love, Mercury Necessity, Mars Boldness, Jupiter Victory, and Saturn Retribution. And the ASC presides in the midst of these, the established *Basis* of the universe.[1]

And [the Lot of] Fortune signifies everything concerning the body.

---

[1]The ASC was the prime point in the horoscope. The houses were counted from it, and the (astronomical) MC degree, if it was wanted at all, was calculated from the ASC. Hence the ASC was legitimately called *Basis* because it was the foundation of the horoscope.

The [Lot of the] Daemon is the ruler of the mind and the disposition and intelligence and all power; sometimes too it has to do with the matter of action.

The [Lot of] Love signifies the desires and longings, [and] things done by choice; it was also instituted [to be] the cause of affection and charm.

The [Lot of] Necessity makes subordinations and anxieties and conflicts and battles, also enmities and hatred and condemnations and all other violent things befalling men in the course[1] of life.

The [Lot of] Boldness was instituted [to be] the cause of boldness and treachery and strength and all criminal acts.

The [Lot of] Victory was instituted [to be] the cause of faith and good hope, and of contest and all fellowship, and, in addition, of enterprise and luck.

The [Lot of] Retribution was instituted [to be] the cause of the spirits of the underworld and all things concealed, also of exposure and inactivity and flight and destruction and mourning and of the kind of death.

The [Lot of] Basis, which is the ASC, was instituted [to be] the cause of life and breath because at the time of birth all that which is generated from the breathing of air draws forth the breath of life at the moment of the water clock[2] that was appointed at birth, which is indicative of all things.

Example. It will be necessary to calculate the Lot of Fortune in the manner previously stated: in the case of diurnal births, from the degree of the Sun up to the degree of the Moon, comprising all the

---

[1] The Greek text has *en genna* 'in the coming forth' where 'coming forth' is a technical term for one of the Moon phases. I have assumed that this is an error for *en genea* 'in the course'.
[2] *Stalagmiaia hôra* 'dripping hour', a good name for a water clock.

degrees of the intervening signs and also those of the ASC, and to cast[S.49] the collected number from the ASC in this manner, by giving 30 degrees to each sign, and wherever the entire number leaves off, the Lot of Fortune must be declared to be there.

For instance, in a diurnal nativity[1] let it be given that the Sun was in the 28th degree of Pisces, the Moon in the 28th degree of Aquarius, [and] the ASC in the 11th degree of Leo. We will count from the Sun to the Moon, it makes 330 degrees; we will also add the 11 degrees of the ASC. Together, all the degrees are 341; we will cast from [the beginning of] Leo; it leaves off in the 11th degree of Cancer. This is the Lot of Fortune.

And similarly [we will calculate] the [Lot] of the Daemon from the degree of the Moon up to the degree of the Sun, they are 30; we will add also the 11 degrees of the ASC; all the degrees are 41. We will cast from Leo; it leaves off in the 11th degree of Virgo; this is the Lot of the Daemon.

Similarly too [we will calculate] the [Lot] of Love from the Lot of the Daemon up to the degree of Venus. The Lot of the Daemon is in the 11th degree of Virgo, and Venus is in the 15th degree of Aquarius; we will count from [the lot in] Virgo to Venus; it makes 154 degrees; adding to these also the 11 degrees of the ASC, we will cast from the ASC [sign] itself, [and] the Lot of Love is found in the 15th degree of Capricorn. By day [do it] thus, but by night the reverse; for example, for the Lot of Fortune we took [the distance] for a diurnal nativity from the Sun to the Moon, but [when we are] reckoning with a nocturnal [nativity we take it] from the Moon to the Sun, and the rest [of the lots] similarly.

In a diurnal nativity it will be necessary to reckon the Lot of the Father by degree from the Sun to Saturn, and to cast the collected

---

[1]The ASC and planetary positions that follow are not hypothetical but are taken from an actual nativity. The date of birth is 19 March 353 at about the 8th hour of the day. See Chapter 31, where Paul mentions this nativity again and gives further details.

degrees, together with the degrees of the ASC, from it,[1] and to look where it leaves off; [and] there will be the Lot of the Father; but by night, the reverse. And if Saturn is found under the Sun beams,[S.50] take [the count instead] from Mars to Jupiter, and [cast] an equal [number of degrees] from the ASC, both for those born by night and by day. But [reckon] the Lot of the Mother by day from Venus to the Moon, and [cast] an equal [number of degrees] from the ASC; but by night, the reverse.

[Reckon] the Lot of Brothers, both for diurnal and nocturnal [births], from Saturn to Jupiter, and [cast] an equal [number of degrees] from the ASC; and the Lot of Children for those born by day or night from Jupiter to Saturn, and an equal [number of degrees] from the ASC; and the Lot of Marriage for male nativities, both for diurnal and nocturnal [births], from Saturn to Venus, and an equal [number of degrees] from the ASC; for feminine nativities, both for diurnal and nocturnal, from Venus to Saturn, and an equal [number of degrees] from the ASC.

{Do the Lot of Injury thus for those born by day: from Saturn to Mars, and an equal [number of degrees] from the ASC; but for nocturnal [nativities], from | the Moon to the Sun, and an equal [number of degrees] from the ASC, and an equal [number of degrees] from Saturn |. The archetypal lot itself is produced for those born by day from the Sun up to Leo, and an equal [number of degrees] from the ASC by day; but for nocturnal [births], from the Moon all the way to Cancer, and an equal [number of degrees] from the ASC. The Lot of Exaltation for those born by day, from the Sun to the 19th degree of Aries,[2] and an equal [number of degrees] from the ASC; but for nocturnal [births], from the Moon to the 3rd degree of Taurus, and an equal [number of degrees] from the ASC. But the [Lot] of the Basis, both for those born by day and

---

[1]That is, from the beginning of the ASC sign.
[2]The Greek text has *Anabibazontos* 'Ascending Node'. Evidently the exemplar of MS **Z** (or its exemplar) used symbols, and the symbol for Aries was misread as the symbol for the ascending node.

for nocturnal [births], from the Lot of Fortune to that of the Daemon or from the Daemon to Fortune; whence, if it is less, to take
the one not surpassing the seventh number,[1] and an equal [number
of degrees] from the ASC.}[2]

24. *TABULAR EXPOSITION OF THE TWELVE HOUSES.*

The beginning and foundation of the twelve houses in every
horoscope is the *ASC*, through which all human circumstances are
discovered. For the ASC was appointed to be the giver of life and
breath, whence it is called *Tiller*.[3] It signifies the time of youth,
which is the first [time of life]. And in it the action of either the bad
things or the good things is made known. In this house[S.51], only the
star of Mercury rejoices beyond all [the other stars]; but whenever
one of the benefic stars or one of the luminaries or the star of Mercury is operative on the ASC, without any configurations with the
malefics, the native is viable and reared, and it will continue his
life in good fortune. But whenever one of the malefic stars is in the
ASC and beholds the Sun or Moon, the native is non-viable or
short-lived, or injured, or emotional, or continued in orphanhood.

The second [sign][4] from the ASC is called *Livelihood* and *Gate
of Hades* and *succedent* to the ASC; sometimes too it signifies the

---

[1]This presumably means that if the two subtractions give unequal results,
the one that is less than 180 degrees ("the seventh number") should be
taken.
[2]The passage in braces is found only in MS **Z** and may be an interpolation. The words marked off by vertical bars do not belong where they are.
[3]In Greek, *oiax* 'tiller, rudder, or helm'. An old epithet of the ASC, cf.
Vettius Valens, *Anthology*, iv. 12, (*ho hôroskopos*), *hos esti zôê, oiax,
sôma, pneuma* 'the ASC, which is life, tiller, body, breath'; and Papyrus
London 130 (Neugebauer & Van Hoesen, *Greek Horoscopes*, p. 22)
...(*H)o d(e) oiax tôn (h)olôn (h)ôroskopos...* 'And the tiller of them all,
the ASC...'. The papyrus contains the horoscope of a native born on the
evening of 31 March 81.
[4]Most of the ancient astrologers used the Sign-House system in which the
entire rising sign constitutes the 1st house, the next sign the 2nd house,
etc. Hence, the word 'sign' is often used for 'house', since the 2nd sign
from the ASC is also the 2nd house from the ASC.

topic of action through the harmony that exists because of the sinister trine [it receives] from the MC$^{S.52}$. When the benefic stars are present in this house, they denote good fortune with the passage of time; sometimes too they indicate those who inherit from others (*sc.*, non-relatives), for this house is the giver of good expectations. But the malefics posited in this house indicate loss of livelihood, and losses of assets, and generally those who are unsuccessful in acquiring property; sometimes too they make emigrants.

The third [sign] from the ASC is the saving up of wealth. But it also signifies the topic of brothers. It is called *Goddess*, the *House of the Moon*, and the *Good Cadent*$^{S.53}$. It is assigned the topic of affection or patronage, and sometimes too it becomes the cause of living abroad because it is opposite to the sign of the Gods, which signifies the topic of living abroad.[1] In this sign the Moon alone of all the stars rejoices. But whenever the benefic stars of the sect are operative there, they declare an increase in livelihood and an acquisition of wealth, and they render the topic of brothers and friends helpful and more sympathetic. They also make those who have many friends, and well-known persons, and those with many brothers; and they bestow favors and gifts from friends and brothers. But the malefic stars posited in this house$^{S.54}$ denote the opposite of these things.

The fourth [sign] from the ASC is called *Under-earth* and *IMC*$^{S.55}$, being the northern angle, signifying the time of old age$^{S.56}$ and the end of living and the wrapping of the corpse and all the things [happening] after death. It is the house of lands and foundations, of parents and of the father, and of the house and dwelling-place, and signifying all [kinds of] household goods, and sometimes too the acquiring of ships and watery places. It also shows the topic of close association with others.

---

[1]Opposite houses share some significations, but note that Paul assigns the *cause* of the affairs of the opposite house to this house.

The [star] of Saturn posited in this house, in sect, indicates rich persons and those who become affluent from middle age [onward]; sometimes too it becomes the giver of things that are found. But whenever [it is] out of sect,[1] [it gives] all kinds of evils. By night, it decreases the [size of] the paternal estate, causes banishment of the father or orphanhood and it indicates a sickly youth; and it is the cause of ill-repute. When the [star] of Mars chances to be on[2] this house by day, it denotes sickly persons and those with the falling sickness[3]; but by night it will lessen the severity; sometimes too, it causes the native to be involved in military service; in addition, it is evil for matters concerning weddings and children; and in general it makes those who are greatly wronged and discomfited by women.

The fifth [sign] from the ASC is called *Good Fortune*, being the *House of Venus*, and when the star of Venus happens to be in it, it rejoices more than all the [other] stars in this house. Moreover, it is the succedent of the IMC angle, and it signifies the topic of children. The benefics[S.57] rejoice in this house and give good childbirths, but the malefics in this house become destroyers of children.

The sixth [sign] from the ASC is called *Bad Fortune* and *Punishment* and *before the DSC* and the *Bad Cadent*, being termed the *House of Mars*. It signifies the topic of injuries. In this house the star of Mars rejoices more than all [the other stars]. The remaining stars, when they chance to be on this house, show themselves to be

---

[1]"Out of sect" refers to a diurnal planet in a nocturnal horoscope or a nocturnal planet in a diurnal horoscope.

[2]Here, for the sake of variety, Paul says "on the house" instead of "in the house." The former phrase refers to the planet's location *on* a two-dimensional diagram, while the latter (and more common) phrase refers to its location in(side) a metaphorical house.

[3]Probably epileptics, although the lexicon calls attention to the fact that Ptolemy, *Tetrabiblos*, iii. 12, speaks of diseases that come from *ptômatismôn ê epilêpsiôn* 'falling fits or epileptic seizures' (Robbins's translation) and thus seems to be drawing a distinction between epileptics and those who fall down because of some other ailment.

idle and weak with respect to the force of their own astrological influences whenever none of the benefics is operative on the upper angle or in the succedent of the ASC.[1] In this house the [star] exhibiting[S.58] the action becomes effective whenever it casts its rays partily upon the MC because this house[2] is harmonious and dexter [to it], standing in trine to the culminating angle. This house signifies the classes of female persons straining in service, I mean female slaves[3] and cattle. But it also causes enmities arising from feminine persons, and also conspiracies and insurrections.

In this house, the Sun indicates one born of a father who is poor or dishonorable or ignoble or exiled; and sometimes too he is bereft of his father. But when the Moon chances to be on this house, it will make the mother a servant or a beggar, or poor or dishonorable, or very small [in stature]; and sometimes too it causes[S.59] bereavement of the mother.[4] In this house, i.e. the sixth from the ASC, Mars rejoices in a nocturnal nativity, and he summons[S.60] [the native] into military service or military glory whenever he is found in a feminine sign and is trine to the Sun or Moon or to the [star] of Jupiter or when it chances to be with the [star] of Venus or else is in trine to her.

The seventh [sign] from the ASC signifies marriage arrangements and extended residences abroad and the maker[S.61] of death[5]; it is called *Anti-Ascendant*. It is also the *setting* [sign, and] it shows the period of old age. When it chances to be in this house by day, the star of Saturn rejoices whenever it is found in its own sign or triplicity or exaltation. For it will make long-lived persons, those fortunate in later life, those of many years, [and] well-to-do; it denotes those who are not injured in their secret places; but sometimes it will make pain in the seat[6], and sometimes it indicates

---

[1]The 2nd house.
[2]That is, the sixth.
[3]Masculine slaves are denoted by the 12th house.
[4]That is, the native's mother will die early.
[5]That is, the *anaeretic* place.
[6]The reference is to those suffering from hemorrhoids, and, in the next

bleeding for those sitting down; sometimes again it encompasses those with a tendency to dysentery or stomach-disorders. And it considerably augments the foregoing increases of sufferings, and especially when it is operating in alien signs.[1]

When the [star] of Mars chances to be on this house, it becomes[S.62] the perpetrator of many evils, sometimes destroying by injuries and sometimes by sicknesses; and it will make those who are unsuccessful in acquiring property, or those who meet their end in some strange, foreign land, or emigrants, or those who live abroad; sometimes too it indicates short-lived persons and those dying violently[S.63] whenever it aspects the Sun or the Moon or receives the application of the Moon, if it is also found without [any] rays from the benefics.

The [star] of Jupiter operating in this house will make those who acquire possessions easily with the passage of time, for this is the angle of late luck; consequently, it bestows advancements late in time. It will also make a fortunate marriage, but few children, and it denotes those who suffer grief because of their wives and children.

Venus possessing the setting angle will make those who marry [considerably] younger women; it shows a trouble-free old age, and it will make an easy death.

The [star] of Mercury will make prudent persons and those who are skilled in grammar, but also those who are disturbed by mental illnesses.

The Sun chancing to be in the setting angle shows persons who live splendidly and rich persons and those who are born of famous fathers whenever it is found in a masculine sign and without [any] ray from the malefics, [and if] the geniture is [also] diurnal.

---

clause, to acute cases where the blood vessels burst when the sufferer sits down.
[1]That is, when it is *peregrine*.

When the Moon is allotted the seventh [sign] from the ASC, it will make [periods of] residence abroad. And if it is found in moist signs, and the geniture is diurnal, it will produce shipowners or steersmen or sailors or those leading a commercial life, constantly wandering about and having ups and downs of fortune.

The eighth [sign] from the ASC is called *Idle* because it is averted from and unconnected with the rising sign; it is also the succedent of the DSC; it signifies the event of death. This house was ordained to be unfortunate; and when the benefics chance to be in this house, they will make profit from deaths, for they give inheritances, and they indicate those who are benefitted by things having to do with death. Not only do the benefics show this moderately, but also the malefics, when they chance to be on this house, will make benefits from deaths; and certainly the Moon too, when it is adding to its numbers[1] and increasing in light, since, after making its course from the conjunction,[2] it is beheld in this house against the visible sky[S.64], therefore it too manifests the advantages [deriving] from death and grants inheritances, especially when it is moving up to the north.[3]

When the Sun chances to be on this house, it shows the banishment or injury or sickness or early death of the father, but in other matters it will be less active. And when the waning Moon chances to be on this house, and without the rays of the benefics, it will make paupers, wretched persons, those who are unsuccessful in acquiring property, and those who are emotional. But when the malefics chance to be here, out of sect, they bring on loss of livelihood and destruction of personal enterprises, and losses, and they cause extraordinary crises; sometimes too they become the causes of a bad death.

---

[1]That is, when its motion is *swift*.
[2]The new Moon.
[3]When its latitude is north and increasing.

When Venus chances to be in this house, it will make the [contraction] of marriage to be delayed; and sometimes it indicates pederasts and sometimes passionate and lecherous persons.

When the [star] of Mercury chances to be on this house, it makes those who are fond of rest, silent persons, recluses, and sometimes thieves or forgers. And it will make stupid persons and those without understanding, or lazy persons whenever it chances to be under the Sun beams or is beheld by Saturn by presence or by the square or opposition position having more degrees than it.[1]

The ninth [sign] from the ASC signifies the matter of gods and dreams and living abroad; it is also the *astronomical*[2] and the pre-MC [house] if one goes from the DSC to the east. It is called the *House of the Sun*, for in this sign only the Sun rejoices. And it is called the *Good Cadent*. When the Sun or Saturn or Jupiter or Mercury have been operative in this house, they bestow favors or gifts or kindnesses from gods or kings; and [these stars] make philosophers and initiates and good businessmen; and sometimes they bestow an office in sacred affairs, or they denote those in charge of sacred affairs; and they do certainly give royal gifts, but they indicate those who live abroad.

The Sun[S.65] operative here with the star of Mercury denotes psychics and dream-interpreters, astrologers, augurs, and in general those who participate in the mysteries. The Moon chancing to be here and making its application to one of the malefics or to the star of Mercury makes those who live abroad.

---

[1]Presumably this means that Mercury is applying to the conjunction, square, or opposition of Saturn.
[2]Rhetorius, Chapter 57, also calls the 9th house *astronomical*, but he may have copied that epithet from Paul. Cumont explains the term by noting that the 9th house is the house of the Sun, but why the Sun should be *astronomical* he doesn't say.

The tenth [sign] from the ASC is called *Midheaven* and *two-thirds of the upward division*,[1] being the southern[S.66] angle and indicating the activities of middle age. It signifies the matter of action and reputation, and rank and standing and precedence, and the father, and the continuation [of status]; [and] it was designated as [the house] showing marriage and male children. When the Sun chances to be in this house, it indicates authoritative and renowned and famous men whenever it is found devoid of any ray from the malefics. It makes those who are born of a noted father. But when the Moon possesses this house in nocturnal genitures, it will make persons who are notable, wealthy, [and] tax-collectors for kings or administrators of cities, whenever it is not aspected by Saturn or Mars either by presence or by square or opposition. You will [also] find that the mothers of these [natives] are well-born.

Saturn holding this house in diurnal genitures, and chancing to be in those signs in which it rejoices, will make occupations connected with watery activities, wealthy individuals and those fond of agriculture, and land-owners and those born of land-owners; and it also indicates owners of buildings. But when it holds this house in nocturnal genitures, it denotes activities in watery places; and it also denotes those having little success and those who do not easily acquire possessions, and those who do not get ahead and who are inactive and unhappily married and have few children and are poor; sometimes too it will make those who live abroad for a long time. or who dwell outside of their own city. and those who wander about for a long time.

When the [star] of Jupiter chances to be present here by day, whenever it is found adding to its numbers[2] or else without any ray from Mars, it indicates those who live on a grand scale, [and who are] magnificent, illustrious, renowned, those entrusted with the

---

[1]*dimoiria tês anô meridos* 'two-thirds [or, double share] of the upward division'. I suppose this refers to the fact that 2/3 of the quadrant from the ASC to the MC is beneath the 10th house, but perhaps there is some other explanation.
[2]That is, *direct* rather than *retrograde*.

affairs of kings or magnates,[1] distinguished and well-known, those having friends among the great, and those who are successful; [but if it is a nocturnal geniture], it will make those who are not well off, neither being obeyed, nor continuing in these actions.

The [star] of Mars holding the top angle (I mean of course the house of the midheaven) in diurnal nativities separates the parents from each other, overturns [the initial status of] those [who have this position], and causes them continue in poverty and straitened circumstances the whole time; and it shows those without an adequate income, and those [who remain] unmarried in their youth; sometimes too it will make those who die violently whenever it is found without any ray from the benefics. But if the [star] of Jupiter and the [star] of Venus are configured with [it], they will have a good old age and they will escape the danger of violent death. Whenever this star is on the MC in masculine signs, in either diurnal or nocturnal [genitures], it will make those who have few children, in conformity with the masculine [sign].

The [star] of Venus being *vespertine*[S.67] in the MC without any aspect from the malefics will make those who live splendidly, high priests[2], fortunate persons, principal priests,[3] city councilmen,[4]

---

[1] Cumont points out in his *L'Égypte des Astrologues*, p. 34 ff., that these "affairs of the king" are for the most part "affairs of state" rather than private affairs of the king himself. The "magnates" are men who were personally acquainted with the king and sometimes entrusted by him with the administration of governmental affairs—something like the cabinet ministers in modern governments. In most cases they were probably members of old and rich families. Those persons with Jupiter fortunately placed in the 10th house acted as administrators either for the king himself or for the magnates.

[2] Cumont, *op. cit.*, p. 116 ff., says these *archiereis* were persons of high rank in the royal court and in the government of the state. If their temples were well-endowed or had ample income, they wore a crown and purple robes (like some of today's orthodox Christian prelates). Their significator is Venus because they wore beautiful clothes.

[3] According to Cumont, *op. cit.*, p. 123, the *neokoroi* were principal priests of the Alexandrian god Serapis, presumably ranking below the high priest but above the other priests and temple attendants.

[4] The Greek word is *bouleutas*, 'members of the *boulê* or Council of 500'

chief magistrates,[1] crowned magistrates,[2] and notables. It also becomes the cause of good marriages and easy childbirths; furthermore, it indicates those who are spoken well of by the multitude, public favorites, and persons who are widely known. When it is *matutine*, it alters the rank of the preceding [positions] and turns it into the opposite[3]; and sometimes it indicates those fond of artistic crafts[4] and sometimes those living in poverty but genteel, as for the most part also those experienced in clean work; sometimes too it denotes musicians or those making their living through sound.

The [star] of Mercury holding the top house will make those who get their living from words or knowledge or letters or deliver-

---

at Athens or of similar councils of leading citizens in other Greek cities. These councils were what we would call 'city councils' today. They conducted most of the business of the city-state. This is probably the function that Paul had in mind, although under the Empire the word was also used to designate Roman senators.

[1] In Greek, *prytaneis*, lit. 'prytany-men' or 'presidents' In the time of the Greek astrologers, the *prytaneion* or town hall of many Greek cities was presided over by a single official who was called *prytanis* 'president' and who was the 'chief magistrate' or actual ruler of the city. In Athens, there was no single ruler; instead, the citizenry was divided into ten tribes (*phylai*). Each of these had a council made up of the 50 leading members of the tribe. Each tribe, in rotation, assumed control of the city government for a period of 35 or so days each year (which was called a *prytany*). So, in effect, each member (*prytanis*) of a tribal council became a city councilman (*bouleutês*) during the prytany when his tribe was in control. Since Paul has just mentioned *bouletai* 'city councilmen', it seems likely that he meant *prytaneis* to be understood as 'chief magistrates'.

[2] In Greek *stephanêphorous* 'crown-bearers' or crown-wearers'. This could mean a priest of sufficiently high rank to be entitled to wear a crown or it could mean a temple functionary who carried the crown of the high priest in religious processions.

[3] This presumably means that the *matutine* position will involve the native in the same occupations or social positions, but at the lowest level rather than the highest level.

[4] *philotechnous*, lit. 'fond of crafts'. Since the significator is Venus, artistic or decorative crafts are meant. Valens, *Anthology*, i. 3.34, explains the word thus: *philotechnôn ē kai technitôn* (*hoion epiplastôn, zôgraphôn, toreutôn*) 'fond of crafts, or craftsmen (such as plasterers, painters, sculptors in relief)'. Of course, by plasterers and painters, he means artists who do decorative molding in plaster and who paint pictures.

ing speeches; sometimes too it indicates supervisors or chief clerks[1] or copyists or notaries or lawyers or legal experts or interpreters or money-changers[2]; configured with Mars, either by presence or by square or opposition, [it makes] liars, atheists, ungodly, sacrilegious persons who rob the god,[3] [and] in addition either poisoners or those knowledgeable about poisons,[4] and forgers or counterfeiters, or armed robbers or murderers, or accomplices in those [crimes], and in general persons of ill-repute, and they will be notorious on account of these things; sometimes too it will make executioners or jailers or mine-foremen[5] or tax-collectors, for indeed the combination of Mars with the [star] of Mercury without the assistance of the benefics always produces perpetrators of evil deeds.[6]

The eleventh [sign] from the ASC is called *Good Daemon*, since it is the house of Jupiter; for when it is present in this house, the [star] of Jupiter rejoices more than all the other stars. It signifies the topic of standing together and leadership, and through these it is also significant of good expectations.

When the Sun chances to be in this house, it indicates the offspring of an honored and rich father, and with the passage of time it will make him happy and one who acquires possessions easily.

When the Moon chances to be on this house, and especially when the birth is nocturnal, it will make [the native to be born] of

---

[1]*skriniarious* = the Latin *scriniarios* governmental officials in charge of official correspondence and records.
[2]*trapezitas* 'money-changers' or 'bankers'.
[3]Those who steal valuable offerings or religious objects from the temples.
[4]The Greek word *pharmakon* means some non-food substance that can be ingested by eating or drinking. Thus it can be translated as 'medicine', 'drug', or 'poison' depending upon the context of the sentence. In this instance it plainly means 'poison', since the significators are Mercury and Mars ("knowledge to do harm").
[5]Miners were generally prisoners or slaves, so mine-foremen were in fact wardens of condemned persons.
[6]Reading with MS **M**: *autourgous* 'perpetrators', instead of . . . *kai eis to kakon axionas*.

an honored and rich and prosperous mother; and it shows the native to be prosperous and elegant whenever it has made an application to one of the benefic stars.

When the [star] of Saturn [is] on this house, in sect, it denotes those who, with the advance of time, achieve those things they desire, but it will make them more idle in their actions and their endeavors. But in a nocturnal nativity the [star] of Saturn holding this house becomes the cause of diminution of things previously owned; and it will make slothful persons and those who are unsuccessful and those who do not easily acquire possessions.[1]

When the [star] of Jupiter holds the eleventh house either by night or by day, it augments the livelihood and places [the native] in [position for] distinction and acquisition of property; and it will make glorious persons and those who gain the upper hand over their enemies; and so for the most part it will preserve the natives free from injury and free from sickness.

The [star] of Mars holding the eleventh house from the ASC in a diurnal geniture indicates loss of livelihood and miscarriages of affairs and changes of places and accidents, and it harms the matter of children. But in nocturnal nativities it brings about the existence of many good things; and it will make those who are deemed worthy of esteem by the multitude and [who have] friends among those in authority.

The [star] of Venus acting here will make happily married persons and those who live decorously, well-behaved and lacking nothing in their livelihood, and prospering with the passage of time whenever it chances to be unaspected by any ray of the malefics.

---

[1] In the Greek text this sentence describing the influence of Saturn when it is out of sect is found at the end of the following paragraph describing the influence of Jupiter in the 11th house. I have moved it to its proper place.

When the [star] of Mercury chances to be in this house, either *matutine* or *vespertine*, it will make those who earn their living from words, and it will help to keep their successes abundant, and it indicates those who increase their livelihood with the passage of time; sometimes too, it is the cause of [personal] excellence, and it denotes those who partake of knowledge.

The twelfth [sign] from the ASC is called *Bad Daemon* and *rising before the ASC*, [and] it is the House of Saturn. In this house, the star of Saturn in diurnal genitures, holding a masculine sign, alone rejoices; and it will always make those who prevail over their enemies and suppress them and those who are occupied[1] with their own affairs, for it indicates lords of a district and rulers and those doing mighty deeds and [who are] tyrannical[2] in their behavior. This house also signifies the matter of sicknesses and childbearing and enemies and male slaves[3] and quadrupeds.

The Sun happening to be in this house shows that the [native's] father will be banished or will die early,[4] and it harms the father through sicknesses or injuries or exile, or it shows quite clearly that the father himself is restrained by poverty, or ill-repute, or low birth,; and it indicates that the natives themselves are unostentatious and poor and needy.

But the Moon [here] shows that the mother is a slave, or of little account, or ignoble, or banished. If it is beheld by a malefic star or if it has made its application to one of the malefics, it indicates that

---

[1]Reading *askholountas* 'are occupied' with MS **M** and the γ family, rather than *aukhountas* 'boasting' with MS **Y** and the δ family.
[2]The Greek word *tyrannos* 'tyrant' means someone who holds absolute power in a city or region, with the implication that he seized power rather than acquired it in what his subjects would have considered to be a proper manner. Here we have the adjectival form *tyrannikos* 'in the manner of a tyrant'. It probably qualifies the preceding word *iskhyropragmonas* 'doers of mighty deeds' to indicate those individuals who seize power in a totally ruthless manner.
[3]Note that female slaves belong to the sixth house.
[4]Lit., the native will become an orphan with respect to his father.

the mother is very sickly, injured, or short-lived. It will make those who are being investigated[1] to be poor and wretched and continually in misfortune.

When the [star] of Jupiter holds this house, it will make uprisings of enemies, and law-suits with inferiors, and loss of the patrimony; however, in the case of slaves and quadrupeds, it is fine and helpful, since it has [influences] very suitable for that case.

The [star] of Mars chancing to be on this house harms the matter of slaves and quadrupeds, and it produces ambushes and plots[2] by servile persons.

When Venus chances to be on this house, it will make those who are made sad by feminine pretenses and those who are disturbed by diseases of the soul, i.e. erotic individuals. And they have sexual relations with slave girls or old women or whores, for the sake of whom they remain in [a state of] childlessness. But if the [star] that receives the star of Venus is configured angular,[S.68] it will make those who have intercourse with slaves and bad marriages, and sometimes too those who are panderers of their own wives.

When the [star] of Mercury holds this house, it denotes thieves, robbers,[3] slanderers, evil-doers, collusive plaintiffs, deceitful persons, and hypocrites; sometimes too it will make[S.69] secretaries[4] or elementary school teachers or interpreters or lawyers.

---

[1]That is, those natives who have this position.
[2]The Greek text has *aitias* 'causes', 'occasions', etc. But Heliodorus's *Commentary*, Chapter 23, has *epiboulas* 'plots', 'treacheries'; Rhetorius, Chapter 57, *epiboulais* 'treacheries'; and Firmicus, *Mathesis*, iii. 4.34 has *insidias* 'ambushes', 'plots', etc. The idea is that masters will suffer violence at the hands of their slaves.
[3]*aphanistai* 'those who make things disappear' or 'destroyers'. Perhaps the *aphanistai* were what we would call 'robbers', 'looters', or 'pillagers', i.e. those who both steal and destroy, while the *kleptai* were 'sneak thieves'. The latter are more commonly mentioned in the astrological literature.
[4]Persons of authority in the government, like today's Secretary of State or the Secretary of Defense.

25. *CHILDREN.*

It will be necessary to look at the 5th and the 11th from the ASC and the top house and the one lying opposite it, which is the IMC, and the Lot of Children,[S.70] and also, in addition to these, the [star] of Jupiter,[S.71] the ruler of its triplicity, and the [star] of Venus and the [star] of Mercury.

And if one place or two or even more are found unaspected by Saturn and Mars and the Sun and the Moon's nodes, the matter of children will be free from pain and sorrow whenever the lords of the aforementioned places or the stars which have been mentioned are themselves not found on the Bad Daemon [12th house] or the Bad Fortune [6th] or the 8th—I am indeed speaking of Jupiter or the ruler of its triplicity, Venus, [and] Mercury.

And if the benefics, or one of the two of them, are found in fertile signs, while the Moon or the ASC or the significator of children are [also] found in fertile signs without any ray from the malefics, this scheme becomes indicative of many children.

But if the [star] of Jupiter is in the 12th or the 6th, while one of the malefics is angular with the [star] of Venus, it becomes the cause of childlessness. But the [star] of Jupiter being ruler of the triplicity,[S.72] while a cadent malefic holds the significator of children, will make those with few children.[S.73]

Venus with the [star] of Mercury in Capricorn or Aquarius holding the 5th house without any help from Jupiter becomes the cause of childlessness, and they hamper conception. Mars in the MC in a feminine sign in a nocturnal nativity will make those having few children; but in the MC by day in a masculine sign it will make those who are childless, and especially as regards male children.

The malefics being in the sign of the Good Daemon,[1] while the Sun together with Jupiter is cadent, indicates those who are childless. When one malefic holds the 5th house [and] the other is with the [star] of Jupiter or the [star] of Venus and they are badly placed, the scheme becomes indicative of childlessness. When the Sun is in the MC [and] Mars or Saturn holds the 5th house, or Jupiter or Venus are badly placed, let this scheme be considered to be [indicative] of childlessness.

But when Jupiter and Mercury have obtained the lower angle, or if one of them is in the DSC and the other in the ASC, they indicate the loss of male children. But the Moon lying in the terms or places[2] of Mercury when Venus is found in Saturnian signs or terms, indicates those having only one child or those who are childless; and their wives[3] are sterile or have only one child. When Saturn and Mercury chance to be angular, they afflict the matter of children. Venus and the Moon, being in the terms or signs of Saturn, or having exchanged the aforementioned positions, will make those who are childless whenever Venus or the Moon chances to be aspected by Saturn or Mars.

But if the scheme is not beheld by one of the malefics, it will surely make those who have few children; and if the previously mentioned schemes chance to be in Aries and Sagittarius and

---

[1]MS **Y** has 'in the signs (houses) that are good', the others have 'in the signs of the Good Daemon', and MS Laurentianus Gr. 28,7 adds the gloss 'in the 9th and the 11th house; however, the 11th house, that of the Good Daemon, is normally associated with children, while the 9th house is not. I have assumed that 'signs' is an error for 'sign'. But perhaps MS **Y** is correct, in which case we should read 'in the Good Daemon (the 11th house) or the Good Fortune (the 5th house)'.

[2]Presumably, the *signs* ruled by Mercury, although the Greek *topois* 'places' normally means '(celestial) houses'. But Heliodorus (Chapter 24) has *oikois* 'domiciles', so perhaps *topois* is simply a textual error in the archetype.

[3]The Greek word *gynaikas* can mean either 'wives' or 'women', so an alternative (but less likely) translation would be 'and women [who have this position] are sterile or have only one child'.

Gemini and Libra, it signifies those having few children; and [if they are] in Taurus and Virgo and Capricorn and Leo and Aquarius, it must be considered sterile$^{S.74}$ and entirely childless; but in the triplicity of Cancer and Scorpio and Pisces, being prolific and having many children and conceiving easily is signified for the stars that are in or bearing witness to the previously mentioned places.

26. *ACTION.*

Because of its quickness,[1] the topic$^{S.75}$ of action is apprehended from the stars that have swift motion—I mean Mars, Venus, and Mercury; but I do not mean that every art and science can be perceived from these three stars. And the houses that are especially serviceable for the presence of these [stars] are these: all the angles and their succedents and the sixth from the ASC—with the culminating sign[2] being particularly preferred among the angular houses, and the second from the ASC among the succedents.[3]

But if none of the previously mentioned stars is placed on one of these houses, nor on the Lot of Fortune, it is proper to inquire [whether] one of them has received the application of the Moon or of the Sun, or whether by chance Saturn, Jupiter, or Mars has made its morning appearance—or, in the case of Venus or Mercury, its evening rising—seven days before or seven days after the birth.[4] For if one of these stars is found that has one or even more of the previously mentioned relations, it is necessary to declare [the quality of] action by taking a suitable characteristic of the force of that star.

---

[1]Here Paul seems to make a distinction between an *action*, which takes place quickly, and a *condition*, which may last for an extended period of time.
[2]The tenth house, which particularly rules action. See Chapter 24 above.
[3]Because the 2nd house is in trine to the MC and is also indicative of money. See Chapter 24.
[4]*Cf.* Ptolemy, *Tetrabiblos*, iv. 4.

But if none of the previously mentioned stars is placed on any one of these houses nor on the Lot of Fortune, you will say [that] this particular matter is inactive.[1]

27. *CADENT [HOUSES]*

While there are four angles[S.77] and four succedents and four cadents, it must be known that sometimes too the cadents are effective, and they produce an action that is not one that happens in accordance with the [usual] astrological signification,[2] whenever one of the stars, posited in one of the cadents, has cast its rays within the space of three degrees[3] [S.78] by trine aspect (which is itself harmonious) either on an angle or a star.

As an illustration, say [that] the ASC is in the 15th degree of Leo and the [star] of Jupiter is in the 16th degree of Aries. Since Leo has the ascending angle in the 15th degree, but also the 9th house or Good Cadent is found with Jupiter being there and casting its rays into the degree following the ASC, it becomes effective.

But we may also make use of another example arising from the [angle] of the ASC as we have prescribed. The MC was in the 15th degree of Taurus, and the [star] of Venus was found in the 16th degree of Capricorn, being in right[S.79] trine to the culminating degree and having cast its rays upon the degree following the top angle. The star was effective, and it became active with regard to the astrological signification. Furthermore, the cadent star is strengthened whenever another one of the stars that is located in an angle that is harmonious to it is effective.

---

[1]*Cf.* Ptolemy, *Tetrabiblos*, iv. 4, ". . for persons with such genitures are for the most part inactive (Robbins's translation)."
[2]This means that a planet in a cadent house but in aspect with another planet in an angle modifies the effect of the angular position rather than producing an effect characteristic of the cadent house itself.
[3]That is, an *orb* of three degrees is allowed for the trine aspect cast by a planet in a cadent house.

The ninth and sixth houses are said to be different from the rest because the ninth[1] is harmonious with the ASC and the <sixth>[2] is configured by trine with the top angle, I mean of course the culminating sign. And the sixth house happened to be more effective because it is harmonious with the culminating angle. For they wanted this one to be the leader of the rest of the angles, just as they also intended the second [house] from the ASC to surpass the rest of the succedents because it is harmonious by trine aspect with the culminating [angle] and because of the acquisition of livelihood from the culminating and the other angles and the significative star making an appearance in one of the angles. But they affirm [that] the maker of the acquisition is shown by the star that is found in [one of] the four cadents of the nativity.

As an example, let it be said that Jupiter is effective in the top house and the [star] of Venus is in right trine to the midheaven [from a position] that is cadent and the sixth house of the nativity. The acquisition is produced by Jupiter, but the maker by the star of Venus; just as if one of the malefic stars, I mean Saturn or Mars, is effective in one of the angles, with Venus being cadent, and, through happening to be in harmony with it, the cause[S.80] arising from the angularity of the malefic star is predicted[S.81] as coming from the pretenses of women.

But in the cadents, the malefic stars become more active for damage and injury when one of the malefic stars happens to be effective on one of the four angles. For the causes of the hurtful situation are predicted through these, and especially when one of the malefic stars is found in the sixth house. But when one of the benefics possesses the sixth house, with no [star] in the MC and none in the succedent of the ASC,[3] it becomes entirely ineffective and inactive and useless and idle for all astrological activity, and

---

[1]Reading *ton enaton* 'the 9th' instead of *to einai ton*.
[2]I have restored *hekton* 'sixth', which has evidently dropped out of the text. As it stands the Greek text is muddled, but the sense is simply that the 9th house is trine the ASC and the 6th house is trine the MC.
[3]That is, the 2nd house.

especially for those actions that are useful for one's livelihood and that can turn into something good.

28. *THE MOTION OF THE SUN AND THE ROUGH CALCULATION OF ITS SIGN AND DEGREE.* ^{S.82}

The Creator of All Things, the Sun, makes his motion from sign to sign, sometimes in 31 days, or 30, or even 29. He advances in each day[1] by one degree more or less, sometimes with one minute, sometimes with one degree and two minutes—at perigee, of course—and sometimes [only] 59 minutes, or 58, or 57. Claudius Ptolemy's *Handy Tables* will furnish the exact degree of the Sun.[2]

To find out easily the position of the Sun for a [particular] inquiry, do as follows: gathering together the days from the first day of Thoth down to the day sought, add to these the constant 156,[3] and from the combined number subtract half of the months that are from Thoth to the one required;[4] and if [the result] has a [full] circle, take it away, and cast the remainder from [the beginning of] Aries, giving 30 degrees to each sign; and wherever the number leaves off by exhaustion, say [that] the degree of the Sun is rather roughly [calculated to be] there.[5] ^{S.83}

---

[1]Here Paul uses the word *nychthêmeros* '*night-day*', which signifies a complete 24-hour period and not just the daytime portion of a day.

[2]Above this statement, MS **Y** has the word *pseudos* 'false!'. Since **Y** is a 15th century MS, the copyist may have been aware that positions taken from the *Handy Tables* were no longer accurate in his own time. However, in Paul's day they were the most accurate obtainable.

[3] Accepting the reading 156 of MS **D** (and Heliodorus's *Commentary*, Chapt. 27) rather than the 158 of MS **Y**. This is very close to the mean longitude of the Sun on 1 Thoth 94 Diocletian (= 29 August 377) as given by Ptolemy's tables (156°02'). See the Commentary for a further discussion of Paul's method.

[4]In other words, take the number of months, divide it by 2, and subtract the integer part of the quotient from the day total. This is a means of adjusting for the fact that the Sun's mean longitude increases by only 59°08' in two months rather than a full 60°. Paul's correction is close enough.

[5]See the Commentary for some example calculations.

29. *THE ASCENDANT:*
HOW IT SHOULD BE CALCULATED.

Multiplying the given hours[1] by 15, add to the combined number the degrees more or less that the Sun had in the nativity, and cast the combined number from the [degree and] sign the Sun is in; and wherever the number leaves off by exhaustion, say the ASC is there. But if it was a nocturnal geniture, while [still] using the foregoing method, cast the combined number from the [degree and] sign opposite the Sun.[2]

If you have the hour from an astrolabe, by day multiply the horary times[3] corresponding to the degree of the Sun by the reported hours, and add the product to the rising times corresponding to the degree of the Sun for the [given] clime.

For the multiplication by 15 is used whenever the hours are equal.[4] But the equal and seasonal hours[5] are got from the astro-

---

[1]In Alexandria the hours of the civil day were measured from sunrise, and the hours of the night from sunset. They were what is called "seasonal hours," since their length varied with the season of the year. Hence, they are unsuitable for use in this simple method because the length of the seasonal hours varies. Nevertheless, some of the early astrologers seem to have given out this erroneous method because we find it in Manilius, *Astronomica*, iii. 218-246, but he, like Paul, is aware that it is incorrect. He refers to it as *vulgatae rationis...ordo* 'a common method of calculating' (Goold's translation) and proceeds to explain why it is wrong.
[2]These ancient methods neglect the difference between the right ascension and the longitude of a point on the ecliptic. The maximum error in the calculated ASC degree due to this is about 5 degrees.
[3]The "horary times" are the actual length of a seasonal hour in "equinoctial times," which are degrees of arc. The modern formula for their calculation is: HT = (arc cos (– tan Decl x tan Lat))/6, where Decl is the declination of the Sun and Lat is the geographic latitude of the place. Ptolemy's *Handy Tables* contain a table that gives the horary times for every degree of solar longitude.
[4]Which would only be the case at the equinoxes. See the Commentary for a discussion of this chapter.
[5]Actually, if you divide the product of the seasonal hours and the horary times by 15, you get the equinoctial hours. The equation is: SH x HT = EH x 15 = Arc ; consequently, EH = (SH x HT)/15 , where SH is seasonal

labe if you divide the combined [number] from the multiplication of the hours by the horary times set forth for the degree of the Sun by 15. But if the nativity is nocturnal, it is necessary to multiply the hours after the setting of the Sun, which are nocturnal [hours], by the horary times set forth for the degree opposite the degree of the Sun, and the resulting amount to be added, not to the rising times set forth for the degree of the Sun in the [given] clime, but to those set forth for its opposite. And in this way it extends the whole amount up to the ASC itself, indicating the degree of the zodiac rising on that night in the same clime, which you also then say [to be] the ASC.

30. *THE MIDHEAVEN.*

It will be necessary to work out the degree of the culminating sign in this manner: having counted the rising times of the signs in each clime from Aries up to the degree of the ASC, [then] cast the combined number from Capricorn, giving 30 degrees to each sign, and wherever the number leaves off by exhaustion, there is the culminating degree.[1]

For example, for the clime of Egypt with the ASC in the 15th degree of Leo, we reckon from the beginning of Aries up to the 15th degree of Leo, and we find the rising times of Aries [to be] 21 2/3, and Taurus 25, and Gemini 28 1/3, and Cancer 31 2/3, and up to the 15th degree of Leo we find 17 1/2 rising times[2]; altogether

---

hours, HT is horary times, EH is equinoctial hours, and Arc is the sidereal time interval (expressed in degrees) from sunrise corresponding to the given number of hours, whether seasonal or equinoctial.

[1] As mentioned in a previous note, this method ignores the difference between right ascension and longitude; otherwise, it is technically correct. In the worst case it would cause an error of 5 degrees in the calculated MC.

[2] This method is not quite right, since Paul has simply taken 15/30 of 35 degrees (the rising time for the whole sign of Leo), which assumes that every degree of Leo rises in 1/30 of 35 degrees; but this is not the case, as the earlier degrees rise faster than the later degrees. The error is not great, but the precise rising time (in his system of rising times) for the first 15

they make 124 1/6.[1] We cast these from [the beginning of] Capricorn, giving 30 degrees to each sign. Four times 30 [is] 120. From Capricorn up to Taurus is [that amount plus] 4 1/6 degrees (and the 1/6 [of a degree] is 10 minutes). We say [then] that the culminating degree [is] in 4 degrees and 10 minutes of Taurus.[2]

But it must be known that the culminating degree does not always fall in the 10th [house] from the ASC due to the inequality of the rising times of the signs, but sometimes in the ninth and sometimes in the eleventh.[3] S.84

---

degrees of Leo would be 17°05', a difference of 0°25'. And the total of the rising times up to 15 Leo would be 123°45' rather than 124°10'. See the discussion of the rising times in the Commentary.

[1] In the Greek text the last clause, 'since Leo. . . . times', is at the beginning of a new paragraph, which is inappropriate.

[2] Paul's result is nearly 6° off, partly due to the inaccuracy of the rising times he used and partly due to his failure to convert the RAMC he found to the longitude of the MC. His calculation yielded an approximate value (124°10') of the Oblique Ascension of 15 Leo. And by adding 270° to this he obtained 4°10', which was the right ascension of the MC, not its longitude (which would have been 6°36'). But the Ptolemaic OA of 15 Leo for Lower Egypt is 127°29', which is equivalent to RAMC = 37°29' and MC = 9°59' Taurus.

[3] Cf. Firmicus, Mathesis, ii. 15,4 & 19,12, who notes that the MC degree is frequently found in the 11th house, but forgets to mention the 9th house. Paul is describing the situation that is encountered by the user of the Sign-House system of house division, in which the 1st house consists of the entire ascending sign, the 2nd house is the next whole sign, etc. In this system, the 10th house is the sign in dexter square to the ascending sign. Now if the 1st degree of Cancer rises in the latitude of Alexandria, the 10th house would consist of the sign Aries, but the astronomical midheaven degree would be about the 15th degree of Pisces, which would fall in the 9th house. Conversely, if the 29th degree of Capricorn rises in that same latitude, the 10th house would consist of the sign Libra, but the astronomical midheaven degree would be about the 17th degree of Scorpio, which would fall in the 11th house.

31. *[THE RULER] OF THE YEAR, THE MONTH, AND THE DAY.*

As many years as the native might live, that many we cast from the rising sign, giving the first year of the native's time [of life] to the ASC and the second to the succedent of the ASC,[1] thereafter the next to the third sign from the ASC, and so on with the rest in the signs that follow until it completes the number 12. And again we give the 13th year to the ascending sign, and wherever the number leaves off by exhaustion, we say the year is there.

Similarly again the month is worked out, beginning from the sign in which the year leaves off and giving to the next signs the required number of months; and wherever it leaves off, there we consider the month [to be].

Likewise also you will work out the day, beginning from the sign in which the month fell, and similarly distributing the number of days that was found to the next signs, e.g. giving to each one day, until the number of 12 is completed, and beginning again from the ones previously set forth and filling out the number; for wherever the number gives out by exhaustion, there will be the day, as in the procedure for the year.

As an example, someone comes to 26 years [of age] who has the ASC in Leo; we give the first year to the ASC, the second to the succedent of the ASC, which is Virgo, and the third in order to Libra, the fourth to Scorpio, the fifth following to Sagittarius, the sixth to Capricorn, the seventh to Aquarius, the eighth to Pisces, the ninth to Aries, the tenth to Taurus, the eleventh to Gemini, the twelfth to Cancer. Having finished the first twelve, beginning again anew we give the the thirteenth to the ASC, which is Leo, the fourteenth to Virgo, and the next ones similar to the preceding, until again we give the 25th to the ASC, i.e to Leo, and the 26th falls in Virgo. Lord of the year: Mercury.

---

[1]The second house.

We look at Mercury, how he is situated in the nativity, and which ones of the stars aspect him, and what is the sign in which the year is that they are beholding, and what [stars] in the nativity were configured with it. We find Mercury, lord of the year, in Aries, averted to the sign in which the year is. But the [star] of Jupiter in Gemini is in right square to it, and Saturn in Taurus is in right trine to it.[1] Since the other stars of the nativity do not make much testimony to it, we will not have even a single prognostication of influences from them.

It will be necessary to work out each year in this way, and to give the first month of the year to the sign in which the year fell, [in this case] Virgo, and the second to Libra, and the third to Scorpio, and you will do the rest [in order] similarly to the foregoing down to the month which you seek to know about.

And the day too is sought by using the same method, [beginning] from [the day on which] the birth took place. You will make [your star] from the sign in which the month fell, giving one day to each sign until the number of twelve is completed, and again giving the thirteenth day to the sign in which the month fell; and you will give [the remaining days] similarly in succession until the number of days is completed.[2]

---

[1] Here we have three more positions from the same horoscope used as an example in Chapt. 23. The birthdate is easily found to be 19 March 353 at about the 8th hour of the day (2 P.M.). Presumably the calculation is for the native's 26th year, which would run from his 25th to his 26th birthday. Adding 25 to 19 March 353, we get 19 March 378, or the month following the day-of-the-week example given in Chapt. 20. While any identification of the native must remain a guess, I believe that this is the horoscope of Paul's son, Cronamon, to whom the treatise is addressed. See Appendix II for the chart itself and also my paper "The Horoscope of Cronammon" *Journal of Research* of the American Federation of Astrologers ,Vol. 5, No. 1 (Autumn 1989): 7-10.

[2] The method of prognostication set forth in this chapter is mentioned briefly by Manilius, *Astronomica*, iii. 537-559, "There are some who approve of an alternative scheme: from the sign at the edge of the rising heavens, which the founders of astrology call the Horoscope, since from that point are measured the hours of day, every class of calculation is made

32. *SINGLE-DEGREE [RULERS] BY TRIPLICITY.*

The single-degree [rulers] by triplicity are obtained thus: you must cast the degrees of the Light of the sect which you have noted from the star which has received [the rulership] by sect by triplicity itself, assigning one degree to each star in the order of the rulers of the triplicities according to sect, not giving [the rulership] for the second time to any star while the star from which the beginning of the distribution was made has not yet received [it] for the second time; and in that one in which the last degree of all of the Light of the sect leaves off, we say that that star rules the single-degree according to the triplicity of the light of the sect. We have made for ourselves the table below.[1] S.85

[See the table on the next page.]

---

both in the divisions of time and in their distribution to signs; the years and months and days and hours start from the same source and are passed on to the following signs. . . (Goold's translation). Ptolemy, *Tetrabiblos*, iv. 10, says "We shall discover. . . . the annual chronocrators by setting out from each of the prorogatory places in the order of the signs, the number of years from birth, one year to each sign, and taking the ruler of the last sign." (Robbins's translation) But he differs somewhat from Paul in his procedure for the months and days. Firmicus, *Mathesis*, ii. 27,3, mentions this procedure, but only as regards finding the ruler of the year.

[1]This difficult chapter can scarcely be understood by itself. However, once you grasp what Paul is talking about, it makes sense. Heliodorus's *Commentary*, Chapt. 34, clarifies the matter, but Heliodorus either had access to similar instructions from some other source, or else Paul's text as he read it was fuller than that which has come down to us. The chapter tells us how to do two things: (1) How to find the single-degree ruler according to the triplicity and sect of the degree of the zodiac in which the Sun is posited, and (2) How to assign the planets to the individual degrees. It concludes with a table of the single-degree rulers. See the Commentary for a complete explanation. The purpose of this table is set forth in the first paragraph of Chapter 33 below.

Table of the Single-Degree Division by Triplicity.[1]

	Triplicity 1		Triplicity 2		Triplicity 3		Triplicity 4	
Sign	♈ ♌ ♐		♉ ♍ ♑		♊ ♎ ♒		♋ ♏ ♓	
Deg.	Diur.	Noct.	Diur.	Noct.	Diur.	Noct.	Diur.	Noct.
1	☉	♃	♀	☽	♄	☿	♀	♂
2	♃	☉	☽	♀	☿	♄	♂	♀
3	♀	☽	♄	☿	♀	♂	☉	♃
4	☽	♀	☿	♄	♂	♀	♃	☉
5	♄	☿	♂	♂	☉	♃	☽	☽
6	☿	♄	☉	♃	♃	☉	♄	☿
7	♂	♂	♃	☉	☽	☽	☿	♄
8	☉	♃	♀	☽	♄	☿	♀	♂
9	♃	☉	☽	♀	☿	♄	♂	♀
10	♀	☽	♄	☿	♀	♂	☉	♃
11	☽	♀	☿	♄	♂	♀	♃	☉
12	♄	☿	♂	♂	☉	♃	☽	☽
13	☿	♄	☉	♃	♃	☉	♄	☿
14	♂	♂	♃	☉	☽	☽	☿	♄
15	☉	♃	♀	☽	♄	☿	♀	♂
16	♃	☉	☽	♀	☿	♄	♂	♀
17	♀	☽	♄	☿	♀	♂	☉	♃

---

[1] I have ignored the two tables in Boer's edition on pp. 86 and 87, which are full of errors; and I have constructed the table above by adding the triplicity numbers to the heading of the table given by Boer in her edition of Chapter 34 of Heliodorus's *Commentary* and correcting the errors in the diurnal column of the third triplicity and the errors in the nocturnal columns of all four triplicities in the table she has given on p. 113, where the planets are more often wrong than right. This may not be the exact form of the table in Paul's autograph, but it gives the same information, assuming that Heliodorus's statement of the rules is correct. The principle seems to be that the triplicity rulers are taken in sequence, but since there are 8 rulers and Venus appears twice in the list of rulers, in each group of 7 in the table, Venus must appear only the first time and not a second time.

	Triplicity 1		Triplicity 2		Triplicity 3		Triplicity 4	
Sign	♈ ♌ ♐		♉ ♍ ♑		♊ ♎ ♒		♋ ♏ ♓	
Deg.	Diur.	Noct.	Diur.	Noct.	Diur.	Noct.	Diur.	Noct.
18	☽	♀	☿	♄	♂	♀	♃	☉
19	♄	☿	♂	♂	☉	♃	☽	☽
20	☿	♄	☉	♃	♃	☉	♄	☿
21	♂	♂	♃	☉	☽	☽	☿	♄
22	☉	♃	♀	☽	♄	☿	♀	♂
23	♃	☉	☽	♀	☿	♄	♂	♀
24	♀	☽	♄	☿	♀	♂	☉	♃
25	☽	♀	☿	♄	♂	♀	♃	☉
26	♄	☿	♂	♂	☉	♃	☽	☽
27	☿	♄	☉	♃	♃	☉	♄	☿
28	♂	♂	♃	☉	☽	☽	☿	♄
29	☉	♃	♀	☽	♄	☿	♀	♂
30	♃	☉	☽	♀	☿	♄	♂	♀

33. *[DETERMINATION] OF THE REQUIRED DEGREE OF THE ASC BY NATURAL* MEANS.[1]

The wise men of the Egyptians conceived the single-degree distribution by triplicity to be useful for getting the precise degree of the ASC, following the triplicities that are proper to the stars and the sects of the Lights for both diurnal and nocturnal nativities, according to the effective single-degree distribution of the triplicity rulership of the star, saying that the degree of the ASC is obtained through the rulership by triplicity of the degree of the Light of the sect.[2]

[1]This chapter explains how to determine the probable ascending degree when only the ascending sign is known or when the estimated ascending degree is not considered to be trustworthy. Hence, it gives a method of rectification of the horoscope.

[2]This paragraph explains the purpose of the preceding chapter and its table of planetary rulers. However, the method is missing and must be

And some have made [another] conjecture, saying that the terms of that star in which the Moon is [placed] must be ascending in one of the signs. But those who have worked out and noted the ruler of the terms of the previous conjunction[1] or full Moon or even the ruler of its sign, in whatever degree of whatever sign each of them is in on the natal day, have affirmed that one of these is the degree of the ASC, and especially the one that is effective by virtue of its predominance in the nativity.[2]

But when the lord of the terms and [the lord] of the sign of either the previous conjunction or full Moon are found to have the same degree, either in one sign or in different ones,[S.86] they definitely signify the discovery of the ascending degree. And some signify their approval [of this] by saying that however many degrees the lord of the terms of the previous conjunction or full Moon is found to have in the nativity, the ASC must have the same number.

But others have worked out the degree of the ASC in this manner: knowing the dodecatemory of the conjunction or full Moon previous to the natal hour, in which sign it fell, and similarly too the dodecatemory of the conjunction or full Moon preceding the day of conception, in which sign it happened to be, and the rulers according to triplicity of their sects, one of these is rather more advantageously[3] posited, and they say the degree of the one that is

---

learned from Heliodorus, *Commentary*, Chapter 35. Essentially the procedure is this: for a diurnal nativity, enter the table with the triplicity and degree of the Sun, note the planet that rules the degree, then locate the *estimated* degree of the ASC in the diurnal column of its own triplicity; if the planetary ruler is the same as that found for the Sun, then the estimated ASC degree is probably correct; but if the ruler is different, then choose the nearest degree that has the same ruler as the Sun. This method offers the astrologer several degrees at various intervals from the estimated degree. He can then use other criteria to help select the degree that best suits the character or the circumstances of the native.
[1]New Moon.
[2]This last method is similar to that explained by Ptolemy in *Tetrabiblos*, iii. 2.
[3]Reading with MS **Y** *epikairoterou* 'more advantageously' rather than with Boer (and MS **Z**) *epikentroteros* 'more angular'.

more advantageous[1] by reason of closeness to birth is rising in the sign in which the ASC is, [namely] the degree rising on the day of birth, the one which rises from the invisible into the visible [part] of the cosmos and steers the birth of the infant. When the lords of the triplicity of the nativity are located out of domicile, they give back the degree of the ASC to those ruling in common according to its triplicity, in the sign in which the ASC fell and especially to the ruler of their sign in the nativity.[S.87]

34. *CLIMACTERICS.*

It happens that the death-bringing and especially dangerous climacterics arise from the encounter by progression[2] of the Sun and the Moon, and sometimes too of the ASC, with the rays of the malefics, either by presence together or by trine, opposition, square, or sextile aspect. And the trine aspect from whatever side they allow to escape from the attacking climacteric without danger. In like manner also the right[S.88] sextile and the right square aspect become harmless, while the left square aspect is constituted more dangerous as compared with the other aspects. But the left sextile or square or the opposition and the *kollésis*[3] that occurs by their coming together by presence must be considered destructive and deadly and especially dangerous for you,[4] with the aspect by left sextile being lighter to bear than the previous[5] aspects.

But also the coming together of the Lights, making a *kollésis* by presence or by an opposition position with the Ascending Node or

---

[1]Again, reading with MS **Y** rather than with the printed text.
[2]Paul refers in this chapter to what are now called *primary progressions* and in particular to *zodiacal* primary directions. These are based solely on the longitudes of the points in the zodiac and take no account of the latitudes of the planets. They are timed by considering the rising times of the signs and allowing one degree of arc to a year.
[3]A *kollêsis*, literally 'gluing together', is a close conjunction or aspect with an orb or 3 degrees or less.
[4]Only MS **Z** has 'for you'.
[5]That is, the 'other'.

the Descending Node,[1] signifies the same thing. And in diurnal nativities, say that the *kollésis* made by the solar progression to the [star] of Mars is especially dangerous. But in nocturnal nativities, say that the *kollésis* made by the lunar progression to the [star] of Saturn signifies a frightful climacteric. And a *kollésis*[S.89] being made to the Ascending Node or the Descending Node by progression of one of the Lights, either by night or by day, must be judged especially dangerous. But the *kollésis* to the Moon arising from the solar progression, either by day or by night, must be judged especially dangerous and death-bringing.[2] Similarly too, the *kollésis* arising from the lunar progression to the Sun, either by night or by day, signifies death-bringing danger.

But always the encounters [of the Lights] made by progression to the stars that are rulers of the sect[3] signify that the climacterics will be transient and not especially dangerous. But it must be watched[S.90] carefully that the out of sect [stars] are happening to be present, in the chronocrative passages[S.92] by transit[S.91], the Sun and the malefic stars in the angles, or with the Moon, the Lot of Fortune, or the [star] of Mercury, or even the Ascending Node or the Descending Node, and especially when the malefics, are moving in their morning rising or even[4] in their stations. But also, in addition to these, it will be necessary to work out the years that are involved, either in the preceding new Moon or full Moon of the nativity that is being investigated or in the squares and oppositions of these, the progressions of the Lights or of the ASC, in accordance with the proper clime.

The employment of the solar or lunar or ascendental progressions[S.93] has this method: we reckon[S.94] from that degree in the na-

---

[1]The occurrence of a conjunction or opposition of the Sun and Moon close to either of the lunar nodes would indicate either a solar or lunar eclipse. And Paul says that this is also "destructive and dangerous."
[2]MS **M** and the MSS of the γ family add 'for you.' See above, where MS **Z** preserves (or adds) the same phrase.
[3]That is, the Sun and the Moon.
[4]MS **Z** alone has 'or even'; the others have simply 'and'.

tivity in which the Sun or the Moon or the ASC is found until it encounters one of the previously mentioned stars by whatever sort of aspect, or until it has made a transition[S.95] from one sign to another, and if then it encounters one of the previously mentioned stars before the transition according to the same sign.[1] With one of the malefics being there, it brings the danger of the aforesaid climacterics more swiftly. But if the transition is made before it encounters one of the previously mentioned stars in the description of the transition, it will fulfill the cause of the climacteric.

As an example, the Sun in the 15th degree of Scorpio, Mars in the 23rd degree of Leo, the Moon in the 6th degree of Sagittarius, the ASC in the 21st degree of Scorpio.[2] We take up first the progression of the Sun and the encounter which it makes with Mars and the Moon by partile *kollesis*; but in addition to these also the progression of the ASC and the *kollesis* which the Moon makes by encounter, either with the Sun or with the [star] of Mars.

We shall begin first with the solar progression. Since the Sun is in the 15th degree of Scorpio; it rises according to the Egyptians in the clime of Alexandria in 35 [S.97] years.[3][S.96] I divide the 35 years by the 30 degrees of Scorpio (and its equal-rising [sign]—I mean Leo); I find that a degree of Scorpio (or of Leo) [is equivalent to] 14 months. But the Sun is in the 15th degree of Scorpio, and Mars in the 23rd degree of Leo. I go from the Sun to the position of Mars 8 degrees.[4] I do 8 times 14; they make 112 months [or] 9 years, 4

---

[1] I don't understand what Paul means by this.

[2] The planets were in approximately these positions at 7 A.M. on 5 November 324, and it is possible that this is Paul's own birthdate, in which case he would have been 53 years of age when he wrote this. But on the other hand, this may be merely a hypothetical example.

[3] The sign Scorpio rises in 35 horary times (degrees of right ascension) according to Chapt. 2. These 35 times are equated to years at the rate of 1 time per year. This measure is mentioned by other astrologers, e.g. Ptolemy, *Tetrabiblos*, iii. 10, and Firmicus, *Mathesis*, ii. 11. Firmicus doesn't bother with the horary times but simply states that the signs rise in so many years, thus referring to what we call "primary directions."

[4] That is, he progresses the Sun from its natal position of 15 Scorpio to 23

months. The Sun being by progression by encounter in the left square, being by light,[1] has made a *kollesis* with the star of Mars and has indicated a death-bringing climacteric. [After] 17 years and 6 months it has made a jump-out from Scorpio to Sagittarius and it has indicated another very dangerous climacteric. But the Sun has made a *kollesis* by progression with the Moon in 23 years and 10 months, [she] being in Sagittarius.[S.98] For the degree [of the Moon] in Sagittarius has 12 months and 20 days. But in the same way also you will make the progression of the ASC, as was said previously of the example, so that this should also be done in every case.

Trismegistus Hermes sets forth [his opinion] in his work *On Climacterics*[2] saying thus: "The revolving [stars] do not always become the causes of evil happenings in human nativities. But they do become the givers of misfortunes, of piratic attacks, of damages, of shipwrecks, of [adverse] legal judgments, or of long and protracted residences abroad. And the climacterics that are prognosticated by stars that are out of sect are effective causes of dangers and misfortunes, but by those that are of the sect, [merely] damages, and such like."

35. *CONFIGURATION OF THE MOON [WITH THE SUN].*

The bonding[3] [S.99] of the Moon occurs whenever she is found to be in whatever scheme by right or left aspect with the solar rays.

Scorpio, where it would be in partile square to Mars in 23 Leo. In modern terminology this is a *converse zodiacal primary direction*. (The corresponding *direct* direction between these two bodies would be calculated by rotating Mars from its natal position of 23 Leo to 15 Leo, where it would be in partile square to the Sun.)
[1]That is by aspect, rather than by presence.
[2]This may be either a separate treatise, as I have indicated, or a chapter in one of the other astrological treatises ascribed to Hermes. So far as I know, this quotation by Paul is the only preserved fragment of the text.
[3]This is a technical term, *syndesmos* 'bonding', which refers to the aspects that form between the Moon and the Sun during the course of the lunar month.

For the Moon is found hastening under bonding whenever she falls within five degrees of the solar rays while hastening into conjunction. And the same thing is produced similarly in the schemes of the full Moon. And similarly, when she is found in [either of] of the two squares of the Sun according to the aforesaid mode,[1] she moves under bonding. And, by the same theory, when the Moon happens to be in either of the sextiles of the Sun, she moves under bonding.

But she makes the loosening of the bonding, whenever by progression she passes the degree of the Sun. And if [after] the loosening of the bonding she meets a malefic, it becomes the cause of many evils; but if [she meets a star] that is stationary or decreasing its numbers,[2] it produces spells of madness and periods of distress and decline and chronic sicknesses; and sometimes too it becomes the cause of injuries that are difficult to survive; and sometimes the [native] is deprived of life. But in most cases the loosenings of the bondings are called grievous; and they are strongly afflicted whenever after the conjunction, the Moon, having been loosened [from the bonding], will make an encounter with Mars; but after the full Moon, with Saturn.

And the effects are produced with respect to helping or hurting when the configurations are loosened after the first or last quarter; helping whenever she moves towards benefics, but hurting whenever she moves towards malefics. But do not let yourself forget that, through the progression made by the Lights, sometimes it will make the *kollésis* by a left square, either to Saturn or to Mars or to the Sun, [so that] presenting the matter of ray-casting, it makes an especially dangerous climacteric, as the wise men of the Egyptians have judged.

---

[1]That is, within an orb of 5 degrees.
[2]That is, retrograde.

36. *THE RULERSHIP OF THE NATIVITY.*

The method of [finding] the rulership of the nativity[1] is apprehended from both the Sun and the Moon when they are found in the effective houses of the nativity. And it will be necessary in a diurnal nativity to look at the ruler of the terms of the Sun or the ruler of the exaltation[2] or the lord of the triplicity, but in a nocturnal nativity the ruler of the terms of the Moon and the ruler of her house and the rest as they are in the preceding method. And when by the previously mentioned methods one star has more votes in comparison with the others and is found in its morning rising angular and in its throne,[3] that one has the rulership of the nativity, and especially if it sees the Light of the sect.[4]

And the effective houses in the matter of the rulership of the nativity are these: the ASC and the MC and the Good Daemon [the 11th]; and in addition to these, the setting [sign], and the one above the setting [the 8th], when these signs happen to be masculine. But by night, the 4 angles and the Good Fortune [the 5th], and the Good Daemon, and the succedent of the ASC [the 2nd], and the sign above the setting. For if the luminescent bodies happen to be in these particular houses, they indicate rulership of the nativity. But if they are remote from the preceding houses, then it will be

---

[1]The Greek term is *oikodespoteia*, literally 'rulership of a house(hold)'. Hence, master of a group of whatever size. In astrology it refers to the dominance of one planet over the others in a specified matter, such as the nativity.

[2]The planet, if any, that is exalted in the Sun sign. *Cf. Tetrabiblos*, iii. 2, where the five modes of dominance are listed as "trine (Robbins mistranslates *trigônô* as 'trine' instead of 'triplicity'), house, exaltation, term, and phase or aspect." Here, only MS **Y** has 'ruler of the exaltation'; MS **M** and the MSS of the γ family have 'ruler of the house', and MS **Z** omits the word altogether. I would be inclined to admit **M**'s reading into the text along with that of **Y**.

[3]A place in the zodiac where a planet enjoys two or more essential dignities. *Cf.* Hephaestio of Thebes, i. 19.

[4]Sometimes called the *Light of the Time*. It is the Sun for a diurnal chart and the Moon for a nocturnal chart.

necessary to look at the ruler of the terms or the ruler of the triplicity or the ruler of the sign of the new Moon that occurred previously or the full Moon.

But if the new Moon or the full Moon that occurred previously was inactive, [it will be necessary to look at] the ruler of the sign of the Lot of Fortune, or the Lot of the Daemon, according to the rulership of the triplicity, or the zodiacal [sign], or the terms, and in addition to these, the ruler of the ASC. And that one[S.100] which may be found ruling these particular houses in the houses previously given, being configured with that one that was shown, will assume the rulership of the nativity.

And the [star] of Saturn taking the rulership of the nativity, if it chances to be well situated, gives the total of the life to be 57 years; but the [star] of Jupiter, 79; and the [star] of Mars, 66; and the [star] of Venus, 82; and the [star] of Mercury, 76. But if the Sun or the Moon has any aspect to the star that is ruler of the nativity, the Sun gives 120 [years], the Moon 108. And when one of the 5 planets[1] assumes the rulership of the nativity and is beheld by the [star] of Venus, it adds to the total time of the life the least of its years, 8; and if it is beheld by by Mercury, 20 years; and by Saturn, well-situated and in its sign, 30 years, but if it is not in its sign, it takes away 30 years of the life. But Jupiter adds 12 years; and Mars, well-situated and in its sign, 15 years, but if it is not in its sign, it takes away that many years.

But this must be judged when the previously mentioned benefic stars are found in the succedents, or under the Sun beams, or taking away from their numbers[2] and beholding the [star] having the rulership: they become ineffective in the taking away or adding of years.

---

[1]This is the only place in the main text where Paul uses the word 'planet'.
[2]That is, retrograde.

That manner which also the ruler of the nativity,[1] having fallen under the Sun beams in the cadent signs, gives of the least restoration the years: Saturn, 30 years, 30 months, 30 days, 30 hours; Jupiter, 12 years, 12 months, 12 days, 12 hours; Mars, 15 years, 15 months, 15 days, 15 hours; Venus, 8 years, 8 months, 8 days, 8 hours; the [star] of Mercury, 20 years, 20 months, 20 days, 20 hours. But the Sun, whenever it occupies one of the masculine signs, gives 19 years, 19 months, 19 days, 19 hours; and the Moon, 25 years, 25 months, 25 days, 25 hours.

37. THE NATIVITY OF THE WORLD.[2]

The nativity of the mortal and earthly World, convenient for the inquiry into genethlialogical learning, must necessarily be placed under the revolving stars, making a beginning of the *apocata- stasis*[3] shining through in the creation of the mortal and earthly World, in which manner also things were made manifest in the placement by degree in their own signs, appointed properly by sect, and in the physical distribution of the parts of the sky.

---

[1] Here the full phrase *ho tés geneseôs oikodespotés* 'the ruler of the nativity' appears instead of simply *ho oikodespotés* 'the ruler'.

[2] Boer notes that this chapter is not found in MS **Y**, nor is it mentioned in the Summary or in Heliodorus's *Commentary*. MS **Z** has only the chapter title and the first few lines, but they are at the bottom of f. 156ᵛ, and several leaves have been removed thereafter, so it is uncertain whether the MS originally contained the whole chapter; however, the text that follows thereafter in **Z** is a translation from the Arabic. Boer points out that this chapter differs both in verbiage and in content from the earlier chapters, which suggests that it may be spurious. For the astrological content, *cf.* Firmicus, *Mathesis*, iii. 1.

[3] This word signifies a 'return' or 'restitution' of things to some former condition. Here it refers to the theory that all the planets will return to their original positions after a considerable length of time, that this will be accompanied by a universal catastrophe of some sort, and that thereafter the sequence of events that occurred in the first period will be repeated. This is sometimes called the "doctrine of the Great Year" and was a belief of the Stoic philosophers. The return of the planets to their original position at some initial epoch was rightly denied by Ptolemy (*Tetrabiblos*, i. 2), but it was unfortunately adopted by the Hindus, who made it the basis of their astronomical tables.

Accordingly, the Sun [is] in the 19th degree of Aries, and the Moon in the 15th degree of Cancer, and Saturn in the 15th degree of Capricorn, and the [star] of Jupiter in the 15th degree of Sagittarius, and the [star] of Mars in the 15th degree of Scorpio, and the [star] of Venus in the 3rd degree of Libra, and the [star] of Mercury in the 7th degree of Virgo, with the Basis[1] rising in Cancer with the degree of the ASC the 15th, having been taken in the 11th nocturnal hour.

This is the nativity of the mortal and earthly World. In these particular signs the stars just mentioned first appeared, having eternal breath situated in the immortal part, whence also these same signs are named their domiciles.

[MS **M** and the γ family of MSS add the subscription "End of the *Introduction* of Paul of Alexandria.]

SCHOLIA

[Scholia are marginal notes in the MSS that were made either by copyists or by subsequent possessors or users of the MSS. They were intended to elucidate obscure points in the adjacent text, but their utility obviously depends upon the knowledge of the scholiast. Most of them are helpful, but in some cases it is plain that the scholiast had only an imperfect understanding of the text. Boer's edition contains 100 scholia collected from the MSS. Some MSS contain few or none; others contain most of the scholia. The words to which they refer are marked in the translation with a superscript S. followed by the number of the scholium.

Few if any of these 100 scholia were present in the subarchetype. Most of them (77) are from the now lost MS γ and are found in the MSS that were copied from it. Of the remaining 23 scholia, 12 are found only in MS **Z**; 3 only in **D**; 2 only in **L**; 2 only in the descendants of the now lost MS β; 2 only in **A** (a member of the γ

---

[1]That is, the ASC, the "foundation" of the nativity.

family); 1 only in **v**; and 1 only in **Y**. Scholium 46 (found in MSS of the γ family) contains an example calculation for the date 16 November 1150; none of the other scholia are dated. Thus, it is possible that the scholia of the γ family were composed in the 12th century. Hence, most of the scholia were probably written in the period from the 12th through the 14th centuries.]

1. Scholium. The [signs] between the seasons are called *bicorporeal*, e.g. Gemini [which is situated] between spring and summer, with spring leaving off and summer beginning, i.e. in the leaving off of Gemini and the beginning of Cancer. And Virgo [is] bicorporeal, since it is between the leaving off of summer and the beginning of Libra, i.e. of fall. And Sagittarius [is] bicorporeal, since [it is] between the leaving off of winter and the beginning of spring in Aries. [And they are called] *bicorporeal*, since they are between two bodies, namely spring and summer. For air agrees with spring, summer with fire, fall with earth, and winter with water. And the fixed signs are said to be hard to cure of a habit and steadfast and not changeable from their own affairs, but remaining in whatever happened to be their situation or temperament [either] hurtful or beneficent.

2. Scholium. It is necessary to look at the allotment of the twelve signs with regard to the lands that are situated [in them] in each nativity, whenever we inquire about the beginning or state of life, dwelling abroad, and property, and reputation, or advantage to have sympathetically, e.g. whenever we observe a nativity that has the Moon or one of the benefics in Aquarius or also one of the stars of the sect posited in the angular houses of the nativity or being found in the triplicity of Aquarius—I mean in Gemini or Libra [or Aquarius]—we say [that the possessor of] that nativity will be most happy in Egypt according to the theory of sympathy because Aquarius dwells near to Egypt.

3. Scholium. And he inquires into these matters in Porphyry in the [chapter on] "The Length of Life" in the beginning of his ex-

planation[1] after two leaves and a half page.[2]

4. Scholium. These *terms* are according to the Egyptians, [not those] from the old book that was found by Ptolemy.[3]

5. Scholium. These terms are according to the Egyptians. They also have a distribution for which Ptolemy did not provide any explanations.

6. Scholium. While there are five modes of rulership of the nativity, there is only one mode of the terms. For the summation [of the terms] of each of the stars from each individual sign into a comprehensive sum shows the times which each one of the five planets gives.[4]

7. Scholium. On "The Length of Life." Whenever the ruler of the nativity is well situated, it then gives the years of life. The ruler of the nativity is the one that is found angular in its own terms or exaltation and in its own triplicity and domicile; and, without more [words], the one that has either all or some of the five [modes of] rulership, and is not retrograde, nor under the Sun beams; but more particularly, whichever one has more relations to the Sun and the ASC when it is a diurnal nativity, but to the Moon and the Lot of Fortune in a nocturnal nativity.

8. Scholium. When you find five [and] five, say [to yourself] "five," namely "five"; again, "five," that is, the first five with the second ["five"], i.e. the "five" from below, they make "ten"; which lies second on the line; third, "6", which, with the first "five" and the "five" from below, with the third [number] "6" make "16".

---

[1]The *Introduction to the* Tetrabiblos.
[2]The MS which the Scholiast had in his hands is unfortunately lost, and as Boer notes, no extant MS of Porphyry's *Introduction to the Tetrabiblos* contains the chapter to which he refers.
[3]*Tetrabiblos* i. 21.
[4]These are what were later called "the greater years of the planets." Vettius Valens, *Anthology*, iii. 16, calls them the "complete" years of the planets.

And so on with the rest.[1]

9. Scholium.[2] The previously mentioned [stars] that rise simultaneously in the zodiacal circle lie under these decans. But the decans also have the faces of the seven stars, which have sympathy with the stars that are in them; e.g. suppose the Sun is in the 10th degree of Aries, in the first decan, the face of Mars; then when we inquire [what] the Sun signifies [with regard to] the mental characteristics, you will find the mind of this [individual to be] especially manly, spirited, combative, fond of weapons, and such like. But again, if the Sun happens to be in the 10th degree of the second decan, the face of the Sun, it signifies that this one is noble in spirit, fond of praise, fond of honor, and not at all combative. But if again the Sun happens to be in the 30th degree of Aries, the third decan, the face of Venus, it signifies that this one is womanly-spirited, feminine in form, especially lewd, lustful, and such like. See then how in only one sign three differences in mental characteristics have been displayed. And the astrological influences are inherent in the decans and their *paranatellonta*[3] and the faces.

10. Scholium. He calls the decans "faces," which are ten-degree divisions. The first has 10 degrees, i.e. 10 once; the second [also has] 10, which makes twice 10, or 20, as was set underneath; the third [has] 10, which makes 30 altogether.[4]

11. Scholium. Since each of the signs is divided into three decans in accordance with the 10-degree division, in the shaping of each decan a face of one of the seven stars appears in which [that star] rejoices just as if the whole sign was its domicile. Let us also

[1]The Scholiast is trying to explain that in the Table of Terms the right-hand number in each column is the sum of the number above it and the number to the left of it on the same line.
[2]Cf. Rhetorius, *Compendium*, Chapter 10, the first part of which agrees with Scholium 9 almost verbatim.
[3]The stars that rise simultaneously with a particular degree or sign of the zodiac in a given latitude.
[4]Again, the scholiast is trying to explain the significance of the cumulative sums 10, 20, and 30.

allow that the approach to this is similar to the aforesaid [approach] to [determining] the ruler of the day and ruler of the hour; for, beginning from Aries, we assign its first decan to Mars because Aries is the domicile of Mars, and the second decan to the Sun, and the third to Venus, and the first decan of Taurus to Mercury, and the second to the Moon, and the third to Saturn, and so on in the same order. Therefore we have set up an easy-to-read table like this.[1]

12. Scholium. [He says] that the seven stars—the planets—are called faces having the same arrangement, taking one force or another according to the three decans in each one of the twelfths.[2] The paranatellonta sympathize with these seven, and they become sympathetic to the three decans; and these same paranatellonta are changed according to the forces of the decans. For just as the Sun, when it is in the [sign] of Aries, clearly has another power in accordance with [that of] the first decan in Aries, which the present chapter states, so again when that same Sun is in the second decan, it takes another strength, which it has clearly in itself and is in accordance with itself. Similarly, the paranatellonta of these have joint power, and they either do evil or good; similarly to these, and in all the thirty-six decans (namely, the faces of the twelve signs), know these same seven planets as being according to themselves, in their own arrangement and their own nature, and if at the same time they alter the [significations] of the decans . . . [the remainder of the sentence is corrupt].

13. Scholium. In Aries, first Mars, as ruler of the sign takes [the rulership of] the decan degrees, being third from Saturn, which is first in the order of the heptazone. For we say this: Saturn is in the first zone, Jupiter in the second, and the rest in sequence. And after Mars, as second [decan ruler] the Sun takes [its place], being fourth in the order [of the heptazone] as we have said; then Venus is third, since it has the fifth place among these.

---

[1] This scholium is in the margin next to the Table of Decans.
[2] Signs (twelfths of the zodiacal circle).

And after that one, the [star] of Mercury [rules] from the beginning of Taurus, since it has the sixth [place] in order; and after it, the Moon. Then again as from the beginning, [from] Saturn down to where the descent and order of the *heptazone* is completed. And the seven planets recur in this fashion in [ruling] the degrees of the decans of the twelve signs. For having taken the beginning from Mars, the progression has been made down to the 7th step, which is that of Jupiter; and then after this is Mars, as [it was] from the other beginning; [and so] again the 8th step is assigned to Mars, and so on down to the 14th. And after that one, Mars again has the 15th, and so on.

14. Scholium. For if by chance Mars holds 5 or 10 minutes of the first degree of Aries, it rules these [minutes] just as it rules the whole first degree, and similarly if any other star holds them, you will say that that star is in the *monomoiria* of Mars.[1]

15. Scholium.[2] The table of the *monomoiria*[3] is useful. [And the following chapters explain] how we must know the signs that sympathize with each other, and whether they are disjunct and averted from each other. And [they are useful] for the knowledge of those that are *homozones*[4] of each other and are lessening their evil, which is when they are found to be in their own domiciles or when they are equal-rising or configured by aspect, and read the 8th and

---

[1] That is, 0°05′ and 0°10′ are part of the 1st degree, which according to the table is ruled by Mars. See also Note 2 on p. 8.
[2] This is a rambling scholium that pertains not only to the Table of Monomoiria to which it is affixed, but also to topics in the next several chapters. It is the only one of the 100 scholia that mentions chapter numbers and also the only one that refers to the *Commentary* of Heliodorus, although it does not mention the author of that work by name.
[3] The single-degree distribution, by which the rulership of each degree is assigned to one of the planets. The word *monomoiria* properly means the 'single-degree distribution', but it is also used to refer to an individual degree to which a ruler has been assigned in this system. The plural of the word is *monomoiriai*, which can mean either 'single-degree distributions' or more commonly 'individual single-degrees'.
[4] That is, signs belonging to the same star, e.g. Aries and Scorpio, both of which are the domiciles of Mars.

the 9th and the 10th chapters.[1] And you will follow closely this table of the *monomoiria* and the commentator[2] who is found [to have written] a commentary on all the [chapters] of Paul [starting] from the half of the 8th chapter. (For the commentary is not found from the beginning [of the book] down to the half of the 8th chapter.) And this table of the *monomoiria* is useful [not] only for the applications of the stars by body but probably also for the applications by aspect. For application is twofold—by aspect or by body. But for the separations of the stars, I do not think this table is useful. But rather, omitting these things, read the 30th part[3] of the *Commentary on Paul*, and look at that carefully and you will know these things. And the 30th [part of the] *Commentary* is on "The Year, the Month, and the Day."[4]

16. Scholium. Gemini sees Leo; therefore the Gemini-Cancer-Leo sextile is good; and in the same manner, the Sagittarius-Capricorn-Aquarius [sextile]; but the other sextiles, i.e. Taurus-Gemini-Cancer, or Pisces-Aries-Taurus, or Leo-Virgo-Libra are not [good]; but [instead] they resemble the opposition and especially the square, of which he also speaks in the chapter after this, the one on the aspects. For the opposition is inharmonious because, even though it is from masculine to masculine or from feminine to feminine, yet when the one is rising the other sets, and on

---

[1]The 11th, 12th, and 13th chapters in Boer's edition and the present translation.
[2]Heliodorus, whose *Commentary on Paul* covers most of Paul's *Introduction*. But the commentary on the first several chapters is lost as the scholiast says, (and there is no commentary on Paul's Chapter 37 "The Nativity of the World," which Boer thinks is spurious).
[3]Part 30 of Heliodorus's *Commentary* is devoted to an explanation of the method of determining the year ruler. It has nothing to do with *monomoiria*. This probably indicates that the sections of the text of Heliodorus used by the scholiast were numbered differently from the text established by Boer. Part 34 of Heliodorus comments on Chapter 32 of Paul's *Introduction*, which deals with a second type of *monomoiria*—the *monomoiria* distributed to the triplicity rulers. Perhaps it is to this part of Heliodorus's *Commentary* that the scholiast refers.
[4]This is the 29th chapter in Boer's edition, but the next four chapters treat the year, the month, the day, and the hour individually in more detail.

this account it is somewhat in the midst of harmony and dishar-mony. But the square [is] from masculine to feminine and from feminine to masculine, and on this account it is entirely discordant. And in like manner, in the case of the hearing and commanding [signs], a harmonious and good sextile is that through Virgo-Li-bra-Scorpio, for the [sign] Virgo commands and the [sign] Scorpio obeys, and [similarly] the one through Pisces-Aries-Taurus. But again, the other sextiles are inharmonious to these.[1]

17. Scholium. Then it is necessary to see whether [it is] *in sect* or *out of sect* and whether it is aspected by a benefic or a malefic or by a member of the sect or not by a member of the sect.

18. Scholium. The [aspects] to the leading [signs] are called *dexter* and those to the following [signs] are called *sinister*.[2] Con-sequently, in those that are more on the right-hand side those hav-ing a greater interval in the *homozones* have greater power.

19. Scholium. The three, Saturn, Jupiter, and Mars, are said to be "revolving," since they go round about and withdraw from the Sun by every distance.[3]

20. Scholium. The three, Saturn, Jupiter, and Mars, for these are configured with the Sun by every [possible] aspect.

21. Scholium.[4] In the case of the three stars, one must conceive

---

[1]Presumably he means that the other sextiles to the named signs are inhar-monious, e.g. Virgo-Libra-Scorpio is a harmonious sextile but Can-cer-Leo-Virgo, Leo-Virgo-Libra, Libra-Scorpio, and Scorpio-Sagittar-ius-Capricorn are not harmonious, etc.
[2]The words *dexter* and *sinister* are the Latin words for 'right' and 'left' respectively and are commonly used in the earlier modern astrological literature.
[3]The three outer planets can be separated from the Sun by any distance, but the two inner planets Venus and Mercury can only separate from the Sun by a maximum of 48° and 28° respectively.
[4]The scholiast sets out to explain the difference between the phases of the three outer planets and the two inner planets, which Paul does not do. However, he explains the phases by referring to the epicyclic theory of

of the morning rising and the evening setting, and the evening rising and the morning[1] setting. And in the case of the two [stars], Mercury and Venus, one must conceive of the morning rising and the evening setting. When the Sun sets, and one of the former, i.e. Saturn, Jupiter, or Mars, rises, it is said to be *acronychal*.[2] Therefore, in the case of the three stars, it is necessary to think of the morning appearance and the evening disappearance. For one does not ever find a morning disappearance and an evening appearance in the case of these three stars.[3] For if it is a morning disappearance, as in the case of the other two, it becomes apparent whenever, with the star in its maximum elongation from the Sun, the star again moves forward, and it goes on until [it reaches] the Sun itself; [but] in the case of those three it is not possible because those stars are not set in motion about the Sun itself; [so] how will they make their morning disappearance with respect to it, when they are at the apogee of the epicycle and separating from it by a large interval. For then, with Mercury and Venus holding the same sign in the center of the epicycle,[4] it will move in the middle of the Sun, whenever from the second station, as they are going towards the apogee of the epicycle, then they make their morning disappearance.

---

planetary motion as used by Ptolemy in his tables. The explanation is necessarily rather technical, and if the reader is not familiar with a diagram of the epicyclic motion, he will find this scholium difficult to understand. It is in fact an astronomical note, not an astrological one.
[1]The Greek text has *hesperian* 'evening', which is wrong. It should read *heôian* 'morning'. Probably the scholiast got confused and inadvertently wrote down the wrong thing.
[2]Modern astronomers would say that the planet is "in opposition."
[3]Because the Sun moves faster than the three outer planets; but the inner planets can move faster than the Sun.
[4]Here, and in what follows, the scholiast relates the phases of the planets to the epicyclic theory of planetary motion. In that theory the "apogee of the epicycle" corresponds to the relative positions of the Earth, Sun, and an outer planet when the planet is conjunct the Sun. At that point in time the planet is invisible. Thereafter, the Sun moves steadily ahead of it in the zodiac, so that it rises above the horizon before the Sun rises, and begins to make its morning appearance. Towards the end of its synodic cycle, when the Sun is approaching conjunction with the planet, the Sun

But this is not done in the case of the three [stars]. For the center[1] of those is made forward of the movements of the Sun,[2] and only then at the apogee of the epicycle the star and the Sun are together, whenever the evening disappearance is made. And after this, with both the Sun and the star being at the morning horizon, the Sun moving into the following parts the center of the epicycle. And the star, going down from the apogee of its epicycle,[3] whenever the Sun stands away on either side by 15 degrees perchance or even 20, then the star makes its morning appearance, going down from the apogee of the epicycle, and making its trine separation from the Sun, the star going down and yet also being in the preceding parts of the epicycle,[4] it makes its station[5]; and, being at the perigee of the epicycle, and with the Sun receding even further, it becomes *acronychal*, as the star sets when the Sun is rising, and conversely the Sun sets when the star is rising.

And with the Sun standing [still] further away, i.e. up to 240 degrees in the case of Saturn and Jupiter, (and 120 degrees in the leading direction), it happens again that the second station[6] is made, with the star going past the perigee of the epicycle and it becomes placed in the same line, where the first station occurred. And there is the first trine, the one at the first station, standing off from the star with respect to the Sun by a *dexter trine*,[7] for it stands

---

sets and the planet, although still above the horizon, becomes invisible because it is too close to the Sun. A few weeks later it emerges from invisibility by rising before the Sun, and the whole cycle begins again.
[1] Here, by 'center' the scholiast means the location of the planet on its epicycle.
[2] By 'forward' the scholiast refers to the fact that the planet steadily falls further behind the Sun from one day to the next. Hence, in the sense of the diurnal motion, the planet is to the right of the Sun, which is the forward or 'leading' direction.
[3] The phrase 'going down from the apogee' means 'moving counter-clockwise in the epicycle from the apogee'.
[4] That is, in the first half of the epicycle where its epicyclic anomaly is from 0 to 180 degrees.
[5] The first station or what we would call *static retrograde*.
[6] *Static direct*.
[7] For example, with the Sun in Sagittarius, Saturn makes its first station

away from it in the leading [signs]. And the second trine is *sinister*,[1] for the star is separated [from the Sun] in the following [signs]. But also with the Sun still moving forward, as it draws nearer to the center of the epicycle, and the star moves forward still, and it comes to be at the apogee of its own epicycle. And then, before the Sun unites [with it] in the middle; and again a conjunction is made at the western horizon, and then it is said to be a disappearance.

For since appearing before, it is now invisible; with the Sun going together with it, it is evident that it is hidden. And [this] is not said of the evening appearance of the three [stars]. Therefore, in view of what has been said about this, in the case of these three [stars], it is pointless to speak of the evening appearance or the morning disappearance, which in the case of the other two [stars] are [actually] perceived and produced.

22. Scholium. It must be known that whenever the Sun is coming along behind[2] the [star] of Jupiter or the [star] of Saturn or the [star] of Mars [and] is distant from them by 15 degrees, those stars are said to be *setting*. And whenever finally it arrives at them partilely, they are said to be *under the Sunbeams*.[3] And whenever the Sun separates from them by 15 degrees or even 10, those stars are said to be *morning rising*. And whenever one of these three is opposing [the Sun], it is said to be *acronychal*. And it is said to be *acronychal* because when the Sun is setting that one appears [in the east].

(static retrograde) in Leo, where it is in dexter trine to the Sun.
[1]Four months later, the Sun will have moved into Aries, while Saturn is still in Leo. Then it will make its second station (static direct), and it will be in sinister trine to the Sun.
[2]That is behind in the zodiac, e.g. if Jupiter were in 25 Leo and the Sun in 10 Leo.
[3]This and the preceding statement are not quite correct. As the Sun moves closer to the planet, the planet is *setting* until the Sun moves to within 15 degrees of it. Then the planet is too close to the Sun to be seen after sunset, and then it is said to be *under the Sunbeams*. This is also called the *evening disappearance*, for the planet ceases to be seen as an evening star.

And in the case of Mercury and Venus, it does not occur thus, but they are always close to the Sun, and whenever they are moving forward[1] they arrive at the Sun. And whenever they arrive at it partilely, they are said to be under the Sunbeams.[2] And whenever they are distant from it by 15 degrees, then they are said to be *evening rising*. And whenever they stand still at the first station and [then] become retrograde, the Sun arrives at them, and whenever it arrives at them partilely, they are said to be under the Sunbeams. And whenever it is distant from them by 15 degrees, they are said to be *morning rising*.

23. Scholium. Especially if [while also being] in sect, they are angular and are situated in their own domiciles. And if not, their [action] is blunted.

24. Scholium. Mercury and Venus do not make a trine or sextile or any [other] aspect to the Sun; for how [could they], when [they are only] 22 and 48 degrees away? But they can sextile each other, whenever one is separated from the Sun on the following side by 22 degrees and the [other] on the leading side by 48 [degrees]. For then they become [separated] by 60 [degrees] or more, which [interval] is a sextile.

25. Scholium. He does not say this well, for it is not possible for these three stars to be occidental to the Sun up to the sinister trine, as when they are in conjunction with it, and then when they are separated from it, because of their seizure by the Sun.[3] And in the

---

[1] From their second station (*static direct*, as we would say today).
[2] Again, the planet is nominally *under the Sunbeams* when it is within 15 degrees of the Sun either before or behind it. But Venus in particular may still be visible until it is within 10 degrees of the Sun either before or behind it.
[3] Paul says an outer planet is occidental from the time when the Sun is in sinister trine to it until the separation is reduced to 15 degrees (at which time it becomes invisible). This seems to be perfectly clear. I think the scholiast is trying to say that the planet is not occidental when it is within 15 degrees of the Sun, but only when it is between 15 and 120 degrees to the left of the Sun, which is merely another way of saying the same thing.

case of [the] two [stars], neither a complete trine to the Sun nor any other aspect can be made.

26. Scholium. For they also become *doryphories* of the Moon, both in the leading and in the following [degrees of] the same sign, for until then we say the star is *morning rising* or *evening [star]*, until the Moon has gone out of the sign in which the stars have made their appearances with respect to it.

27. Scholium. That is, in the ASC or in the MC. For these are said to be advantageous houses.

28. Scholium. Whenever one [star] has the Sun in its own domicile, then it is said to be its *domicile-receiver*.

29. Scholium. For after the first station,[2] it retrogrades more in the zodiac, moving in the epicycle down to the perigee, during those days that it is retrograding, moving daily [only] some [few] minutes in the zodiac.

30. Scholium. For when it has been direct as far as 4 signs, it then becomes stationary; and after that it begins to retrograde, with the Sun proceeding into the 5th or even the 6th sign after it.

31. Scholium. When they are going up from the perigee of the epicycle after the acronychal [phase], up to the apogee, where also the second station[3] is made.

32. Scholium. For it does not become stationary in the 120th degree, but either in the 82nd or the 84th. Wherefore it is also said to become stationary anomalously; and this comes about because of

---

[1]For example, if the Sun is in Taurus with Venus, then Venus receives the Sun by domicile and is also present in the same sign with it. The Greek technical term, which has no exact modern counterpart, is *oikodektôr* 'domicile receiver'; it is a special instance of *dispositor*.
[2]The modern term is *static retrograde* (SRx).
[3]The modern term is *static direct* (SD).

its swift mean motion. For it moves in the epicycle LA.[1]

33. Scholium. Because the degrees in which this one makes its station are not determined.

34. Scholium. So that it produces a square to it; for after the station that is produced in the 82nd degree, [and] after 8 degrees [more] it produces 90 [degrees], [which] will be square the Sun.

35. Scholium. For in this table the greatest *prosthaphairesis*[2] of these becomes evident from the tables of the anomaly.

36. Scholium. These are called *phases* (appearances) because at this elongation from the Sun they appear.

37. Scholium. More of the whole light being produced.

38 Scholium. For the astrological influences, either good or bad, act directly within the three-degree [interval]. And if it is a nativity, [they act] in the age of childhood. And if it is a good [star] with which it unites, [it predicts] good things; but if it is a bad one, bad things.

39. Scholium. For example, if both the star and the Moon are towards the north or the south, and if the [Moon] is towards the south, and the [star] is towards the north, and the aspect will occur, the astrological influences will be entirely altered, either by presence or by aspect, if they are not towards the same wind,[3] by a perpendicular from the star that is present with her.[4]

---

[1]The letters LA refer to a particular diagram of epicyclic motion, such as one of those in Ptolemy's *Syntaxis*.
[2]The maximum value of the Equation of the Center, which is the deviation of the true place in orbit from the mean place. The word *prosthaphairesis* is a technical term that means "addition or subtraction'.
[3]By *wind*, he means 'direction'.
[4]This scholium appears to express a contrary opinion both to that of Paul and to Ptolemy, *Tetrabiblos* i. 24, which says that the two bodies must have the same latitude in the case of a conjunction, but that in the case of

40. Scholium. For in every action and in every nativity and in every *katarchê*,[1] they say it is impossible to foretell [anything] without [considering] the separation and the application of the Moon.

41. Scholium. The knowledge, he says, from this, and which wind will blow and whether [it will be] unsettled or calm. And you will know, he says, from the application or separation according to the triplicity. For not only by body is it said to be an application or separation, but also by aspect. Therefore, whenever it makes an application to or a separation from a star in the first triplicity, Aries, Leo, and Sagittarius, *Apeliotes* [the East wind] will blow. And whether the wind is good or bad may be determined from the star toward which it moves. And in the second [triplicity], that which is through Taurus, Virgo, and Capricorn, [it will be] *Notos* [the South wind]. And in the third, that which is through Gemini, Libra, and Aquarius, [it will be] *Lips* [the Southwest wind]. [But] in the fourth, [which is] through Cancer, Scorpio, and Pisces, [it will be] *Borras* (the North wind). And by another theory, he says, these things about the winds were stated more accurately.

42. Scholium. That is, each day of the week is [ruled by] one of the stars.

43. Scholium. The fourth is taken, or an equal number of days, because of the leap-years.

44. Scholium. That he is speaking of Egyptian years, and because of this he says to add the fourth. For the Greeks and the Alexandrians reckon the fourth [as part of] each four-year period.

---

an aspect, it doesn't matter "because their rays meet at the center of the earth." However, I incline to think that the text of the scholium is faulty and that the scholiast intended to repeat Ptolemy's opinion.

[1]The Greek word *katarchê* means 'beginning'. It is used to designate either an Election or Horary chart, since each of these is a 'beginning'—the former being the beginning of an action and the latter the beginning, i.e. the moment, of a question.

And because of this, in the Greek years [it is] not [necessary] to add the fourth, since it has already been added.

45. Scholium. The remaining from the summation of the days of the 1/4th and of those of the month [are] 20 days. And the 28th according to the Alexandrians, according to us is the 26th, with the 3 being added, both of October and of December and of January.[1]

46. Scholium.[2] It must be known that the fifth day of the week was the beginning of the [first] year of Diocletian, which indeed had its beginning after the completion of the leap-year. And since it had the fifth [day as its] beginning, and the taking-away of the days by weeks is necessary, to take the beginning from the first of the week, [it is] necessary to add 4 days, which happen to be reckoned from the first down to the fifth. And since time revolves by weeks, as we also speak of the weekly periods, and for 52 weeks amounting to a year except for one day, and according to whichever day of the week the year begins with, according to that same one then it also takes the last [day]; it is [therefore] necessary from the 52 weeks that are being omitted to keep back the one surplus day. And if the year began from the first day of the week, the surplus one itself is also the first one of the week, as of the 52 weeks, if the year begins from Sunday, it is completed on Saturday. And the following year begins on Monday; and if the year begins on Monday, Monday will also be the surplus [day] according to the first [day] of the completed weeks. And if [it is] Tuesday, Tuesday; and so forth.

It has also then produced the beginning from the [first] year of Diocletian from the fifth day of the week. And since from the first

---

[1]The "3 being added" refers to the fact that the months named have 31 days in the Julian calendar and hence advance the weekday at the beginning of the next month by 3.

[2]Here the scholiast attempts to explain Paul's procedure for finding the day of the week from the calendar date. For a clearer explanation of the method, see my Note 2 to Chapter 20 and the discussion in Section 2 of the Commentary below.

down to the fifth there are four days, it is necessary that after the surplus of the year and these have been included, which this one[1] terms 'general', so that the beginning of the week is taken. And this one took only two and not four, because after these the months are made double, however many they are from the beginning of the year, these running after the completion [of the previous] year, and not only the ones that have been completed, but also the month that has not yet been completed.

And since the others receive the doubling according to the instruction, the ones that have been completed and the weeks completing all fourths, having two surplus days, which must also be combined with the day which is surplus from the year; and it was not necessary that the one that is not yet completed be doubled, so that at the same time he could double it in the same lines (?), he distributed the four general [days], which we mentioned to be taken from the beginning of the week and the two that he called 'general', and the remaining two received the doubling, although not of this of the days that are, but of the general [days] because the first year begins from the fifth [day] and not from the third. For if he had taken two general [days] from the third and this would not ever have received doubling.

And because he has this (?), he will show the finding of the present day to be concluded by this same method, for of the 6659 year, which is the 867th [year] from Diocletian, the fourth of these is found to be 216, and all the days after the 867 being added and the two 'general' [days making] 1,085; these I divide by 7. The remaining days of the stars [are] 7.[2] And since the month is November of the said year, and the day of it is 16, and there are three months from September to this, and these being doubled make 6,[3]

---

[1]Namely, Paul.
[2]The calculation is 1085/7 = 155; hence, as we would view it, the remainder is zero. But the ancients had no zero, so the scholiast uses 7 instead.
[3]The Alexandrian year began at the end of August, and the Byzantine year began in September, so the scholiast counted from September to November, which is three months as he says, so that in this instance the Alex-

and also taken one beyond the 30 days of October because that month has 31 days,[1] and there are also according to us the 16th of the month, according to the Alexandrians the 19th, the whole makes 36,[2] which also dividing by 7, I have 5 days remaining. And [this] is the day of the week today—the fifth.[3]

Therefore, we have taken two 'general' [days] in this [calculation] and not four because we doubled November according to the surplus. For from Sunday, from whence the numbering of the days arises, down to the fifth [are] four days, for of the 'general' [days] are also the two according to him. And if you will examine the first year from Diocletian, as in the following, you will find the method to be true. For if you take the first day of the first year, the surplus [day] from the 52 weeks, if it was the first [day] of the week the beginning of the past first year, and it was first. And if <this first would have been last, and the> one following, would be certain to be Monday.

But according to the present method, if we have added the doubling of the first month, although not yet completed, and whichever day of it is one. The fourth, if of the week the beginning of the following happened, which is not true. For if the first is terminated in Sunday, having begun from this, the next begins on Monday, so that in vain the doubles of the said month were taken because these

---

exandrian month is also the third month, Athyr.

[1] The month of October and the number of its days should not enter into the calculation at all.

[2] How he arrived at 36 is not clear (unless he has added 6 to the 30 days mentioned in connection with October). And his statement that dividing it by 7 leaves 5 is wrong – it leaves 1. But curiously enough his statement that 5 is left gives him Thursday for the weekday, which is correct. The true Pauline calculation would have been $7 + 6 + 20 = 33$. And dividing this by 7, the remainder is 5 or Thursday.

[3] The Byzantine date is 16 November 6659 = 16 November 1150 A.D. It was in fact a Thursday. The corresponding date in the Alexandrian calendar would have been 20 Athyr 867 Diocletian, one day later than the day that the scholiast gives. Here we have the date when the scholium was written—Thursday 16 November 1150. And since this scholium is found in the γ family of MSS, it perhaps serves to date that family of MSS.

two are not of the month, nor are they reckoned, but of the beginning of the year, of the general [days] also, from which he took the two months, and the two he disregarded in the doubling up of the incomplete months. And the four general ones are taken because of the convenience of the starting-points, so that from the first of the week, the days are brought forth, just as Ptolemy also taught us to do from the apogees of the stars and of the Sun.[1]

47. Scholium. Through this and the multiplication by 13, since reasonably the dodecatemorion is 2 1/2, and the multiplication of it by 12 may become twelve times the 2 1/2 [or] 30. Hence, if the 30 are multiplied by 12 and they are distributed to the 12 signs by 30's, the generated 360 [degrees] do not come to the same sign, but they arrive at the one before it; e.g., if the 30th [degree] of Aries is multiplied by 12 and they make 360 and they give 30 to each sign, the number will leave off at the end of Pisces and not touch Aries. And then the dodecatemorion is produced more plainly, whenever from the same [sign] it falls into the same [sign]. And so that this may occur, the multiplication is by 13. And thirteen times 30 [makes] 390, and they fall again into Aries.[2]

---

[1] As Neugebauer points out in his commentary on Scholium 46: "Der Scholiast hat offenbar nur eine sehr dunkle Ahnung, warum die Formel des Paulus funktioniert, deshalb die langen Umschreibungen." [The scholiast obviously has only a very dim idea of why Paul's formula works; whence the long paraphrases.] Neugebauer goes on to say that the reference to Ptolemy and apogees is inappropriate, but it seems to me that the scholiast is just saying that the days of the week are counted from the first day, just as Ptolemy counts the mean anomaly of a planet from its apogee. But this is an unnecessary remark, and taken in its entirety the scholium does more to obscure Paul's method than it does to explain it.
[2] The scholiast has followed Paul's method, but in fact both of them were in error. The dodecatemorion is a twelfth of a sign or 2 1/2 degrees. If the first dodecatemorion of Aries is Aries, then the last dodecatemorion must be Pisces. And if we multiply 27 1/2 by 12, we get 330, which is the beginning of Pisces. But if we multiply 27 1/2 by 13, we get 357 1/2, which is near the end of Pisces; and consequently 11/12 of the last dodecatemorion of Aries will be Aries instead of Pisces. This is obviously wrong, and it is hard to understand why neither Paul nor the scholiast saw the falsity of multiplying by 13. It is interesting to note that

48. Scholium. Thus Trismegistos Hermes names his own treatise, in which he spoke about the Lots, as they perhaps related to necessary and useful things. For [the treatise] about these Lots was written by Hermes in the book called *Panaretos*. And in it he gives their astrological effects; he says then "seven Lots" for the number of the seven stars; and naming the Lot of the Sun, Daemon; and that of the Moon, Good Fortune; and that of Jupiter, Victory; that of Mercury, Necessity; that of Venus, Love; that of Mars, Boldness; and that of Saturn, Retribution.

And it must be known that there are other Lots besides [those of] the *Panaretos*: [the Lots of the] father, and mother, and brothers, and children, and spouses, and many others; however, Paul did not set forth all of them.[1]

49. Scholium. For as we take [the degrees] from the Sun to the Moon in the following direction, so also [we take] the [same degrees] from the ASC up to where the degrees from the Sun to the Moon terminate. For I cast these same from the ASC, and I add the 11 [degrees] of the ASC to the 330, not as those that are also of the Lot of Fortune, but because the reckoning from the beginning of the sign of Leo is easier to make.

50. Scholium. A star is *under the Sunbeams* whenever it is within 15 degrees of the Sun, but if it goes beyond 15, then it is not said to be *under the Sunbeams*.

51. Scholium. Found in this [house], but not being under the Sunbeams; for then it brings the greatest good to the native; and likewise, if it is not there, but another of the benefics [is]. If indeed Mercury is badly configured here, being afflicted by an aspect of Saturn or Mars, or if one of them is found there and it aspects the

Rhetorius says he tried this method (multiplying by 13) and found by experimentation that it does not give the correct answer.
[1]Heliodorus gives many more in several lists that are evidently derived from different sources. See Chapter 22 of his *Commentary*, and its translation in Appendix I below.

Sun or the Moon, the opposite will happen.

52. Scholium. For indeed from the MC down to the second house is five signs,[1] in which a trine is observed; therefore the MC to the second house is a trine aspect, but it is [an aspect of] the MC towards the leading [signs] (and the second [house] towards the following), wherefore it is also called a *sinister [trine]*.

53. Scholium. The cadent[2] of the MC above the earth will go in the [direction] from the rising to the setting,[3] for the cadents are so taken; but [the cadent of] the IMC in the [direction] from the setting to the rising.[4]

54. However, not finally, since the Moon is wholly in the house place. For, assume too that the Moon is in this [place]; and if one of the malefics is found there, all of the worst things previously mentioned [will occur]; however, if none of the stars is there, it is necessary to ascertain by which [stars] the sign is aspected, and thus the good things will appear middling and the evil things middling. But this [will] also [be the case] in all the houses when no star is present.

55. Scholium. Because of the inclination of the sphere, the IMC always falls further to the north.

56. Scholium. They say that it makes the astrological effects [to occur] in old age whenever it receives the foundation [house] in the nativity. And in action it shows it to be done very slowly. If then, they say, the benefics are present in the IMC, [they produce] the aforesaid good things, and in conformity with these he will become old, and he will be buried by his familiars, and he will be an inheritor; and likewise if it is aspected by benefics, especially in sect. However, if one of the malefics is found, it will not become

---

[1]Counting both ends of the interval, as was the old custom.
[2]The 9th house.
[3]That is, from the easterly to the westerly direction.
[4]Hence, from the westerly to the easterly direction.

entirely bad. For Saturn rejoices in this [house?], especially if it chances to be found in sect in the nativity. And it produces the greatest things from middle age [on, viz.] wealth and windfalls; but if it is found out of sect, [it is] bad, for being found in that condition, it makes a diminution of the paternal property.

57. Scholium. Especially the star of Venus; and if any malefic is found, the malefic is not such a one because of the goodness of the houses, but it becomes *anaeretic* for the [native's] children.

58. Scholium. For whenever a benefic is in the MC casting its rays by trine into this house, a practical person is born.

59. Scholium. And if a trine aspect is cast by the benefics, it signifies that she was helped by a rich man and not set free.

60. Scholium. And if it is also not aspected by benefics, not even thus, it increases great evils, if it is not out of sect; and similarly, if Saturn [is] not found there in sect, since the evil [stars] rejoice in evil things. But if indeed the malefics are found there out of sect, he says that they produce the characteristic evils of the house, e.g. wounds and subversion by female persons.

61. Scholium. And the end of life, and about exposure of a child, and the foetus,[1] and other things in addition according to the stars ruling the house. And it does its good things after the prime of life.

62. Scholium. And especially if it is without the joint aspects of the good stars, e.g. whenever Mars is configured with the Sun or the Moon, or it receives the application of the Moon, then it wounds [the native] with many kinds of illnesses. And if [it is] also without any aspect from the good [stars], then it also makes short-lived persons and those dying violently. Finally, you will know the agent of death from the signs, for if [it is] in wet signs,

---

[1] Or 'pregnancy'.

e.g. Aquarius[1] or Pisces he will be drowned in water; but if in a hot [sign], e.g. in Leo, through fire; and if it is in armed signs, e.g. Sagittarius or Scorpio, through swords; and if it is in animal [signs], e.g. Capricorn, Leo, [or] Taurus, by animals. And it not only makes these things, but it also indicates poor and unstable persons and those living abroad.

63. Scholium. For always when Mars is found with the Sun or the Moon, it makes great evils.

64. Scholium. Therefore it begins forthwith to appear new.

65. Scholium. And if in a nocturnal nativity the Sun is found there with Mercury, i.e. in such a way that Mercury is towards the beginning of the ninth house, and the Sun is towards the end of the seventh, so that it is under the DSC; for otherwise it is not possible for these to be in a nocturnal nativity;[2] [it makes those who are] unsteady in dreams and unfaithful to God, doing nothing that is steadfast.

66. Scholium. Due to the inclination of the sphere, the MC above the earth is always towards the south; therefore, the south is said to be the mid-day [direction] because the culminations are generated at it and the circle through the poles; for this reason, it is said to be the mid-day [direction]. And since the MC above the earth is more southerly, it is necessary that the angle below the earth[3] be more northerly; and therefore, he terms the one in the fourth the "north angle."

67. Scholium. Having a western appearance. For this also comes to the MC, when it is at its greatest elongation from the Sun 48 degrees; for some times around the south, the MC is not distant from the horizon by 90 degrees.[4]

---

[1]Note that the ancients associated the sign Aquarius with water rather than air.
[2]The scholiast proposes something that is astronomically impossible.
[3]The IMC.
[4]Here, the scholiast has confused Venus's maximum elongation from the

68. Scholium. For if a sign is in the twelfth house, having as its ruler a star, e.g. Capricorn or Aquarius having Saturn, and Saturn is in one of the four angles, it makes these things, when Venus is in this [house].

69. Scholium. According to the configuration of the rest of the stars; and it is necessary to understand this in the case of every star.

70. Scholium. For all these houses are said to contribute to [judging the matter of] children.

71. Scholium. Behind [this] I was intending to write that the good [stars] for the giving of children [are] ♃ ♀ ☿ ☽ and the triplicity ruler of ♃, and the angle of children; and the evil [stars are] ♄ ♂ ☉ ☋ ♌. Synopsis of the [chapter] on Children: and one must examine the 5th, 11th, [and] 12th houses, and see if some of the aforementioned stars, ♃ ♀ ☿, are there and the triplicity ruler of ♃ and the Lot of Children. And as Heliodorus says, "when the Moon is also found in the aforesaid houses or in aspect with them, they give children, and especially in [signs] of many children. But if the ☉ or ♄ or ♂ holds these houses, there will be childlessness.

72. Scholium. Whenever Jupiter chances to be in one of the [signs of] the triplicity of Aries, Leo, [and] Sagittarius, for this [is the triplicity] by day of the Sun and by night of Jupiter; [or of the triplicity] of Taurus, Virgo, [and] Capricorn, which is [the triplicity] by day of Venus, but by night of the Moon; [or of the triplicity] of Gemini, Libra, [and] Aquarius, [which is the triplicity] by day of Saturn, but by night of Mercury; [or of the triplicity] of Cancer, Scorpio, [and] Pisces, [which is the triplicity] by day of Venus, but by night of Mars; and if the nativity is diurnal, its triplicity ruler is said to be the diurnal lord of the triplicity, but if by night, the nocturnal [lord]. Therefore, it is recommended to look at what sort [of signs are] the sign of the MC and the IMC and those [signs] that are succedent to them, and to say this, the

---

Sun with the arc from the DSC to the MC.

[sign] of the Good Daemon and the [sign] of the Good Fortune, whether it is one that is of many children or few children, then next to see of what sort [are] the stars in them and what kind aspect them. For if [they are] benefics, Jupiter namely, Venus, [and] the Moon, and the ruler of the triplicity of the [star] of Jupiter, they show many children, and if the Lot of Children [is] in these [houses], and if [it is] without the aspect of the others, [it denotes] not only this but also fruitfulness.

73. Scholium. And [you may learn] about the signs of few children and many children and no children from the book of Sahl,[1] the barren signs ♍ ♑ ♌ - and ♉, [those of] few children ♈ ♊ ♎ and the signs of many children ♋ ♏ and ♓. And [also] in Paul's *Introduction*. But also [in the book] of Timaeus[2]; he ... and ... [*the remainder of this scholium is lost*].

74. Scholium. For all of these it is necessary to look at the Lot of Children and the ASC, in what kinds of signs they are—in [signs] of many children or no children, or few children—and with what kinds of stars, and if [they are] in the said four houses, especially when the four good [stars] Jupiter, Venus, Mercury, [and] the Moon are rulers, and to a lesser degree the rest; and if a benefic is in the fifth [house] or aspects it, for this is indicative of children, since it is also said to be [the house of] conception.

75. Scholium. What [kind of] action and technical skill the native will be [involved in]. Wherefore it is also necessary to look at

---

[1]Sahl ibn Bishr, Abû ꞌUthmân—a learned Jewish astrologer of the first half of the ninth century who wrote in Arabic. He was known in Western Europe as Zahel and was the author of five books on Horary and Electional Astrology that are known in Latin translation. Some or all of these may also have been translated into Greek. Probably the reference is to Book I of the *Introduction to the Judgments of Astrology*, of which the Latin translation was printed at Venice in 1493. See the English translation by James Herschel Holden, *The Introduction to the Science of the Judgments of the Stars* (Tempe, Arizona: A.F.A., Inc., 2008)
[2]An early Greek astrologer, cited by Vettius Valens, and therefore probably of the first century A.D. or perhaps even of the first century B.C.

which of the three stars is in the 9 houses,[1] and more particularly in the 10th and the 2nd; for the 10th is more the ruler than the 2nd. And when you find one of these stars having more dominant houses than the others, declare the actions and the technical skills [of the native to be] according to the action and energy of that one.

76-1. Scholium. Venus [indicates] the fine arts, e.g. playing the *cithara*,[2] dancing, but also painting, and working in ivory, and embroidery, and all those things that are proper for women; and if it holds the more dominant houses, the MC and the 2nd, [the native] will go after those that are the most dominant and esteemed, and if [it holds] the other [houses], the cheapest and plainest of these by diminution.

And if Mercury is found in these houses, it indicates the more capable learned men [and] clerical workers.[3] And it also signifies this, that when the benefic is in a cadent [house] trining either a benefic or an angle, it will recover its own power, and it becomes more energetic if it was also angular; and the angular [position] gives the strength of propitious influence; and the [star] in a cadent [house] trining the agent of good gives [it]. And it produces a similar [effect], but somewhat less, and if the other has been angular, but in its rising. For the one that is in a cadent [house] being trined by it is strengthened, and if the one that is angular is a malefic [and] aspects the one that is cadent, it yet rather weakens it and makes the energy of the benefic weaker.

76-2. Scholium. Otherwise—In the matter of action the more dominant house is, in the angles, the one that is culminating, and in the succedents, the House of Livelihood;[1] the one then of the three

---

[1] Namely, the four angles, the four succedents, and the 6th house (because it is trine the MC).

[2] An ancient stringed instrument, the ancestor of the modern guitar.

[3] The Greek word *grammatistas* means those who work with written documents. This covers a broad range of occupations from high officials in charge of government departments to simple "clerks" who perform routine tasks dealing with letters, records, etc.

stars, Mars, Venus, or Mercury, that is effective in the matter of action and its house work together in the magnitude of action; e.g. in the MC or in the House of Livelihood, the [star] of Mercury bestows better and honest arts and crafts, e.g. sophistical, rhetorical, clerical, [or] educational; and in the more inferior houses, writers of speeches and pleas for the law-courts, legal experts, [or] elementary schoolmasters. And the [star] of Mars in the stronger houses makes generals, or mercenary soldiers, or goldsmiths, but in the inferior [houses] butchers or locksmiths. And Venus in the stronger [houses] makes painters, *cithara* players, weavers of embroidered garments, and in the inferior houses it makes stage performers, mimes, and such like.

And if the three stars, Venus, Mars, [and] Mercury, are in the active houses, [the native] will then be skilled in many arts and crafts rather than an expert in that particular art or craft of the principal star that holds the dominant house. And whenever the 9 houses become effective with the presence of the three stars, Mars, Venus, [and] Mercury, or one of the three, then the rest, e.g. the one having the application of the Moon or of the Sun or the one that is morning rising [will predominate].

77. Scholium. When the benefics are in the angles or the succedents, they have been shown to do their good things more strongly, but the malefics do their their bad things. And now they show that it is possible for those that are in succedents to denote their characteristic things, just as if they were in angles or succedents.

78. Scholium. For the trine is [an aspect] of 120 degrees. If then there are 117 degrees, it is also called a trine, e.g. if one is in the sixth, which is the cadent of the DSC, it throws a ray to the tenth, since it is trine to it, and that is the MC.

79. Scholium. In the cadent of the DSC in the preceding

---

[1]The second house.

[house], being in the sixth house, the Bad Fortune, if indeed Taurus is on the MC.

80. Scholium. The cause through the malefic will be misfortune or war.

81. Scholium. The maker is denoted [to be] through women or through words whenever Mercury is in the cadent, for wars and misfortunes are produced through words and women.

82. Scholium. Wishing to teach about the ASC and the other angles, of which the ASC is first in every *katarche* and nativity, and it is also said to be the *basis* and the preface—and not only of the angles, but also of the rest of the houses[1]; he takes up in advance [how to find] the place of the Sun, for without this it cannot be known which degree the ASC has.

83. Scholium. For the quadrant from 5 1/2 Pisces down to 5 1/2 Gemini, because of the Sun's being in its apogee then; for the apogee of its eccenter is in 5 1/2 degrees of Gemini, and it rotates through it in 94 1/2 days; but the [arc] from 5 1/2 Gemini down to 5 1/2 Virgo through 98 [days], as the apogee moves through 187 days, and the perigee through 178 1/4.[2]

84. Scholium. From the degree 10 of Taurus down to 15 Leo, as he says there, [are] 104 degrees 50 minutes; the remainder from the semi-circle of 180 degrees [is] 75 [degrees] 10 minutes, to begin from 15 of Aquarius down to degrees 10 of Taurus, which is also the MC, as the 3 oriental signs and 14 degrees 50 minutes, but the two occidental signs and 15 degrees 10 minutes, and 6 seasonal hours on each side; and always to take the MC then according to

---

[1]The ancient and medieval astrologers calculated the MC from the ASC, not the other way around as we do today. Hence the ASC was in fact the *basis* of the rest of the houses.
[2]What the scholiast is (or ought to be) trying to say in the last clause is that the Sun moves from 0 Aries to 0 Libra in 187 days, and from 0 Libra back to 0 Aries in 178 1/4 days. But as Neugebauer notes (ed. Boer, p. 139), the text makes no sense as it stands.

the equality of the hours on each side. And the houses are reckoned and distributed according to the number of twelfths on each side. Because it may happen that [the number of] the twelfths on each side are equal, i.e. 3 and 3, since also the seasonal hours always happen to be 6 and 6 (and equinoctial if it does <not> chance to be 4 1/2 and 7 1/2 or 7 1/2 and 4 1/2.)[1] And this happens when Capricorn or Cancer is on the MC.[2]

Then also the tenth house itself is placed in the MC, and if with the hours always being equal on each side, according to which the culminating sign on the MC is also taken from the equinoctial circle, and the sections of the equinoctial [circle] through which the rising-time of the semi-circle is generated, they are always equal on each side; but if when there is more of the quadrant, and when less [of the quadrant], the twelfths are not equal on each side, but either the oriental [signs] are more than three, as there are more than 90 degrees by 14 [degrees] 50 [minutes], and the occidental [signs are] less or else vice versa. Then the culminating [sign] is not the same as the 10th house. But if the oriental [signs] are more, it is found in the 9th [house] and not in the 10th. But if the occidental [signs] are more, in the 11th.[3]

85. Scholium. For example, Jupiter in the 12th degree of Aries, in the [by] triplicity table the *monomoiria*[4] [single-degree ruler] is [the star] of Saturn; for the 12th [degree] of Aries [is] of this [star] according to the correctly made table and similarly in the rest. And when I find in which degree of the triplicity the star [is], I look to see whether [it is] in its own [*monomoiria*] or in that of another and whether that star is a benefic or a malefic and aspected by benefics

---

[1]The text actually has '4 1/2 and 4 1/2, and 7 1/2 and 7 1/2', but the scholiast meant to make both pairs add to 12, as Neugebauer observes (ed. Boer, p. 144 n.3). In the translation I have corrected the error.
[2]As Neugebauer notes (ed. Boer, p. 144 n.4), this statement is false.
[3]The scholiast is pointing out that the MC degree can sometimes fall in the 9th or the 11th house when the Sign-House system of houses is used.
[4]Reading *trígônôi kanoni monomoiría* 'triplicity *table monomoiria*' instead of *trigônikôi kéntrôi monomoiría* 'triplicity *angle monomoiria*'.

or malefics. And thus it appears that if it is in its own *monomoiria* of the triplicity, [it is] good, and if [it is] in good houses [it is] better still, and if it is also aspected by benefics, it is best of all; but if all this [is] the reverse, [it signifies] the opposite.

86. Scholium. If both of the stars are also in the same degree, we look at their *monomoiriai* [single-degree rulers] by triplicity, and if both of them are found to be close to the ASC, certainly then the ASC is thus apprehended, and also if by chance they are in 22 or 23 [degrees] of different signs; and if [the degrees] are not the same, but one is in 22 [degrees] and one is in 16, then the one having more reasons for dominance will take charge of the determination.[1]

87. Scholium. The Sun in the 8th degree of Cancer, the ASC in the 23rd degree in Cancer;[2] I look then to see if the 8th degree of Cancer, which the Sun holds, is the *monomoiria* by triplicity of some particular star, and I find by the aforementioned method that it is of Venus; for Cancer is the 4th triplicity, the 8th degree has lying beside Venus in the vertical [column] in the table. Since then this has been found, that one is the lord of the place of the Sun, i.e. Venus. Therefore I look also in the ASC degree, the 23rd of Cancer, where nearby the [star] of Venus has the *monomoiria* by triplicity according to whatever sign,[3] either in the same 23rd [degree] or in one close to it either greater or less. And I find that there is [one only] one degree from it. For the ascending degree, the 23rd, and the monomoiria by the triplicity of Venus in another [degree of the] sign, i.e. in Cancer itself, is found [to be] the 22nd.

---

[1]The purpose of this scholium is to expand on Paul's rather skimpy instructions for rectifying the ASC by using the table of *monomoiria* rulers by triplicity. The degree numbers 22 and 23 refer to the same example mentioned in Scholium 87.

[2]These positions are the same as those given in the example in Heliodorus's *Commentary*, Chapter 35. Evidently the scholiast had both Paul's *Introduction* and the *Commentary* open before him when he wrote the scholia. And in fact he has merely summarized part of what Heliodorus says.

[3]He means "for each sign of the triplicity."

Therefore, the 22nd [degree] of Cancer is the ASC [degree] and not the 23rd.

And the second method from the Moon alone, either by night or by day, is worked thus. It is sought in which sign the Moon is, then, whenever it is found, it is sought, whose term it holds, i.e. that degree [it is in], whose term it is. And they look for that star, whichever [single-] degree by triplicity it has rulership over that is near the roughly [-determined] ascending degree more or less; and the one that is near [to it] by more or less, I say that that one is the ASC; e.g. in the aforesaid example, the Moon is found in the 23rd degree of Virgo in the terms of Mars, I look in the ASC sign to see where Mars has its *monomoiria* by triplicity, i.e. the same 23rd degree of Virgo and in the same example. And so there the 23rd [degree] was the ASC [degree]; and I find this in the 22nd [degree] of the second triplicity according to the setting forth of the table. This then [is] the one rising. Therefore the [two] methods are in agreement.[1]

88. Scholium. For the sextile from the leading [signs] [is] midway between good and evil.

89. Scholium. For example, if Mars is out of sect. For if Mars in a diurnal nativity aspects the ASC, [it is] very bad, but if in a nocturnal nativity, [it is] middling. And it is also necessary to look at

---

[1] The scholiast has found that Mars is the *monomoiria* by triplicity ruler of the 22nd degree of the earth triplicity according to one version of the table found in the *Commentary* (ed. Boer, p.114), but not according to the table in Paul's *Introduction* (ed. Boer, p. 86). Furthermore, he should not have sought the location of the degree ruled by Mars in the earth triplicity, but rather in the water triplicity, where the ASC is; and there it rules the 23rd degree according to one table (ed. Boer, p. 113) in the *Commentary*, but the 25th degree in the other table, and the 22nd in Paul's table. The modern reader should ignore the scholiast's demonstration, since it is confused; and in general the two methods (one using the Sun's degree and the other using the Moon's term-ruler) would not agree. Furthermore, all of the Greek tables, both Paul's and Heliodorus's have errors. (See p.45 n.1.)

the *epembaseis*.[1]

90. Scholium. Whenever the sextile is made by one degree and partilely. For instance, the sinister sextile kills, if it is not blocked by the presence or by some aspect of a benefic; and if it is sinister, and it is not yet partile and is equal-sided,[2] but is lacking a few degrees, then the aspect is said to be by *kollêsis*, with another *kollêsis* being there in addition to the one just mentioned. For these are the intermediate times of the leading and the following [signs]; so great times they will pass through, and the climacteric will be generated within the partile *kollêsis* of the star or the aspect. For a *kollêsis* of such a kind, and in the method according to the length of life, they give the times of life, as Ptolemy has demonstrated in his [chapter] "The Length of Life" putting the *anaeretic* [place at the] beginning of Gemini and the beginning and *aphetic* place from Aries, putting the times of life according to the separation.[3] For however far it is until the degree of Gemini makes a *kollêsis*, so far then may the years of life be attained. The *kollêsis* then is also beside that one, whichever is also said to be there by progression.

91. Scholium. *Epembasis* is whenever each of the 7 stars makes its return to its own domicile.

92. Scholium. They term it *epembasis* whenever in revolutions [of a nativity] [those] possessing the disposition of the nativity, moving out the times from the ASC, we shall arrive at a sign. For *epembasis* is said of that year according to that sign. If then the year chances to fall out in the angles of the nativity, according to the advance of time and into the Lot of Fortune, of course of that in the nativity. For it is also necessary to notice the angles of the na-

---

[1]Literally, 'advance', but see Scholia 91 and 92 below.
[2]This expression is used by both Ptolemy, *Tetrabiblos*, iii. 9, and Vettius Valens, *Anthology*, ii. 38, to refer to partile *oppositions*, apparently referring to the fact that the aspecting planet in a partile opposition is 180° measured *either way* from the aspected planet. Here, however, it seems that the scholiast may simply be using it as a synonym for 'partile'.
[3]A reference to the examples given in *Tetrabiblos* iii. 10.

tivity or the Lot of the Daemon, or then it was the Ascending Node or the Descending Node, and especially if the [stars] are stationary or they are found to be morning rising [stars], the evil is extended at that time. Just so too if they fall into [the place of] the new Moon and the full Moon, the one generated previous to the time of the nativity, or in the squares or oppositions of these.

93. Scholium. A meeting by a progression is that [produced] by casting a ray, or whichever one is from the following [signs] according to the rising times, and the motion of the stars in longitude from the leading [signs] to the following [signs] by aspects and *kollêsis*.

94. Scholium. For if a star at the time of the nativity is in the following [signs], and the Moon or the Sun is in the following [signs] and they make an aspect to the star, and it is not yet partile, but for five or six or four degrees the aspect is completed, whenever also it becomes partile and emerges through the intervening times, then we say a meeting is produced by progression. And whenever the Sun or the Moon or the ASC chances not to be by aspect but by [actual] presence for the precise meeting, then we shall also say the same thing.

95. Scholium. It is called *exalma*[1] whenever the Sun or the Moon is about to pass from one sign into [another] sign, and it leaves some degrees, [here] e.g. 15.

96. Scholium. For to each rising [degree] they gave a year, i.e. 12 months.

97. Scholium. Multiplying these by the 12 months, and it makes

---

[1]The Greek word means 'distance' or 'interval'. Neugebauer explains (ed. Boer, pp. 145-146) that the *exalma* of a degree is obtained according to Balbillus (CCAG VIII.3, p. 104, 14-19) by multiplying the rising times of the whole sign by 2/5 and calling the result months. The fraction 2/5 is simply the ratio of 12 months divided by 30 degrees. The scholiast evidently misunderstood the term, for his scholium is not helpful.

420; then I divide the 420 by the months, and it makes 14.[1]

98. Scholium. Sagittarius rises in 31 [and 2/3] times. These [multiplied] by 12 are 380 with the 2/3. For twelve times 31 [is] 372, [and] twelve times 2/3 [is] 8, for 2/3 of the 12 [is] 8. I divide the 380 months by 30. For each single degree they amount to 12 months [and] 20 days. For twelve times 30 [is] 360; there remain 20 months. They make 600 days; I divide these by 30, and for each degree they amount to 20 days.

99. Scholium. And this other bonding [is] at the Ascending Node and the Descending Node. For bonding is now said whenever it is 5 degrees before the conjunction with the Sun, or the sextile [to the Sun] whenever it is crescent, or when it is square, whenever it is at its quarter, or gibbous, whenever it is in trine, or whenever it is opposite and it is full Moon. And these [configurations] are sinister whenever the Moon is in the following [signs] and the Sun is in the leading [signs]. But whenever after the full Moon the Moon goes towards the Sun, it is said to be also aspected on the dexter side, so that it is in the leading [signs], and the Sun is in the following [signs], and again it is said to make a bonding when it is 5 degrees before trining or squaring or sextiling, and after the completion of the aspect, whenever it is aspected partilely, and then it is separated a little bit, [and] it is said to dissolve the bonding [after] 5 degrees.

100. Scholium. A star of whatever sort receives in its own triplicity or terms the Part of Fortune or that of the Daemon or the ASC. If then this star is in the aforementioned houses, i.e. in the succedent of the ASC or in the DSC or in the MC or in the others which he said, not being in those of the lights or of the new Moon or of the full Moon, and in aspect with the Lot of Fortune or that of

---

[1]Paul divides 35 by 30 and then (mentally) multiplies by 12 to get 14 months. The scholiast avoids the fraction 35/30 by multiplying the 35 rising times by 12 months and then dividing their product by 30 to get 14 months.

the Daemon, the one that is received in its own place, that one will take the rulership of the nativity.

APPENDIX I

HELIODORUS'S COMMENTARY ON PAUL

[excerpts]

22. The Names of the Seven Lots and the Things that they Signify.

"First, the Lot of Fortune, which must be calculated..." [a reference to Paul's *Introduction*, Chap. 23]

Since in the preceding section we have already mentioned the method of finding the lots, well, now we shall deliver it. And first we shall begin with the Lot of Fortune, since this god [the Moon] produced things rather more related to those things here [on earth], increasing and decreasing matters; wherefore, also that most divine one, I mean Hermes the Thrice Great, will assign it [the Lot] to the Moon for its own.[1] And then after that one the [Lot] of the Good Daemon, since from this we shall be able to perceive the customs of the soul and intelligence and purpose, just as from the [Lot of] Fortune [things] about the body and things having to do with the body.

And with regard to those things especially, the greatest power of divination resides in knowing the customs of the soul and the pas-

---

[1]Firmicus Maternus tells us in *Mathesis* iv. 4 that Abram said that the Lot of Fortune was the lot of the Moon.

time of the body; and he said this, how the soul is governed according to the order in it, that has come from above, and how the body and the things having to do with the body, and he said simply, it meets all the things that are not in us. For the sake of this, the [Lot] of the Daemon and [the Lot] of Fortune should be sought out before all the [other] lots; but he also stated another cause, that because of this the [Lot] of the Daemon and [the Lot] of Fortune should be cast, since from them we shall also cast all the others; we were not able then to cast out the rest of those not cast. After that then these things were well directed, we shall go into what was set forth, and we shall seek out the method through which the Lot of Fortune is cast.

For it is necessary to look at which sign and which degree the Sun is in according to the time of the nativity, or simply to say in every matter that is taken in hand, and similarly in what sign and in what degree the Moon is, and also in addition to these the ASC, in what sign it is and in what degree; and, when these are found, if the nativity is diurnal, then to measure the distance in degrees from the Sun to the Moon, and then with this number that is found to connect with the number that is found in the ASC, then thus to cast [it] from the ASC, giving 30 degrees to each sign and then to look into which sign will fall the number that is found into which degree, and to say that there is the Lot of Fortune.

For the sake of an example, let the Sun be in the 12th degree of Gemini and the Moon in the 28th degree of Aquarius and the ASC in the 10th degree of Libra in a diurnal nativity, then I measure the distance from the Sun to the Moon, since the nativity is diurnal. Then I take [the sum] of the 12 Gemini in which the Sun was and the 28 of Aquarius where the Moon was; it makes 40 degrees,[1]

---

[1]This procedure is of course wrong! Heliodorus has **added** the degrees of the Sun to those of the Moon and got 40 degrees when he should have **subtracted** them and got 16. Suppose that the Sun had been in 28 Gemini and the Moon in 12 Aquarius. By his procedure you would have added 28 to 12 and gotten 40, just as in the example in the book. Plainly this is nonsensical.

then the signs in the middle I multiply by 30, and there are 7 in between Gemini and Aquarius; 7 times 30 is 210; and I combine [them] with the those of the signs in which the Sun and Moon were; it makes 250; and I combine the 10 of the ASC, and it makes 260; finally, I cast from the ASC, giving to the sign of the ASC, I mean Libra, the first 30, and 30 to those following as far as Gemini, for 8 times 30 is 240, the remaining 20 I give to Gemini, and I say that the Lot of Good Fortune is in the 20th degree of Gemini.[1]

But if it was a nocturnal chart, the opposite of this; for I measured the distance, i.e. from Aquarius to Gemini from the Moon to the Sun, and I took 2 degrees of Aquarius and 18 degrees of Gemini, which the Sun traveled; it makes 20;[2] then I measured the distance in between of 3 signs, which is 90 degrees; and I added the 20 of the Sun and the Moon and the 10 of the ASC; it makes 120; I cast from the ASC, giving it the first 30 [degrees] and thus with the rest [of the signs] down to the 4th sign from Libra, finally nothing, and I said this: that Capricorn is the Lot of Fortune in the 30th degree;[3] and thus for the Lot of Fortune.[4]

But in the [case of] the Lot of the Daemon, the other way around, for in a diurnal nativity from the Moon to the Sun, but in a nocturnal one from the Sun to the Moon; again, these must be measured from the ASC, casting the combined number, and wherever the number falls, say that the Lot of the Daemon is there, just as was said in the case of the [Lot of] the Good Fortune; and thus one must say about the Lots of the Good Daemon and the Good Fortune.

---

[1] But it isn't! It should be in 26 Gemini.
[2] Here he has taken the number of degrees from the planet to the end of the sign in each case and added them together. This is incorrect.
[3] The final result is incorrect. The Lot of Fortune in this example should be in 24 Capricorn.
[4] We see from these examples that Heliodorus was not much of an arithmetician. In trying to give an easy-to-follow explanation of how to find the distance between the Sun and the Moon, or vice versa, he set forth two methods that give incorrect results.

It remains for us to inquire into how the remaining lots are cast, beginning first with [the Lot of] Love. For it is necessary to see in which sign and in which degree Venus is and to calculate the middle distance, in a diurnal nativity, from the Lot of [the] Daemon to the degree of Venus, and in a nocturnal [nativity] the other way around, from the degree of Venus to the Lot of [the] Daemon; then to add the [degrees] of the ASC and to cast [the sum] from the ASC and to see in which sign the number falls, for there is the Lot of Love.

And the Lot of Victory will be found thus: in a diurnal nativity, count from the Lot of the Daemon to the degree of Jupiter, then add the [degrees] of the ASC, then cast according to the method given previously for the other lots, and wherever the number will leave off, say that there is the Lot of Victory.

And measure the Lot of Necessity in a diurnal nativity from the degrees of Mercury to the Lot of Fortune, in a nocturnal [nativity] the other way around, then add the [degrees] from the ASC and cast from [it].

And measure the Lot of Boldness in a diurnal nativity from the degrees of Mars to the Lot of Fortune, but in a nocturnal [nativity] the other way around; and similarly, adding the [degrees] of the ASC, cast from [it].

And [measure] the Lot of Nemesis in a diurnal nativity from the degrees of Saturn to the Lot of Fortune, but in a nocturnal [nativity] the other way around, [i.e.] from the Lot of Fortune to the degree of Saturn, [then add the degrees of the ASC and cast from it].

And these are the seven lots that were written in the *Panaretos* by the divine Hermes the Thrice-Great, which Paul set forth here.

It must also be known that there are other lots, aside from [those] in the *Panaretos*, that are called [the Lot] of the Father and of the Mother and of Brothers and of Children and of Marriage and of many others. But Paul did not set forth all of them, for indeed I note that he did not set forth the Lot of Travel Abroad[1] or [the Lot] of Business or [the Lot] of Commerce and other such [lots], but only [those] of the Father and the Mother and Brothers and Children and Marriages, which are necessary [lots], and he says that if you want to cast the Lot of the Father, they reckon from the degree of the Sun to the degree of Saturn in a diurnal nativity, but the other way around in a nocturnal [nativity]. And if Saturn is under the Sun beams, reckon from Mars to Jupiter, both by day and by night. For if the Lot of the Father falls in a good sign, where there are benefic stars, or Saturn is found to be angular, and plainly besides the sign is well disposed, the father is illustrious and fortunate; but if the sign is not found thus, say the opposite.

Reckon the Lot of Brothers both by day and by night from the degree of Saturn to the degree of Jupiter together with the degrees of the ASC, and the Lot of Children the other way around (from Jupiter to Saturn); add the [degrees] of the ASC and cast from it.

And they measure the Lot of Marriage in a male nativity from Saturn to Venus, but in a feminine one the other way around—both by day and by night from Venus to Saturn, and of course with the addition of the degrees of the ASC.

And from all of these it is shown to us that in general the number is produced from either one star to another, as was said in the case of the [Lot] of the Daemon and the [Lot] of Fortune—for there, the number was produced from the Sun to the Moon and from the Moon to the Sun—but also as in the case of the Lots of the Father and the Mother, etc.—or from stars to lots or from lots to stars, as was said in the case of the Lot of Love and [the Lot] of Necessity and the others, both in a diurnal and in a nocturnal nativity; in the case of [the Lot] of Love and [the Lot] of Victory, in diurnal nativi-

---

[1]Reading *xeniteias* 'of travel abroad' with the **â** family of MSS instead of *xenias* 'of hospitality' with MSS **LA**. There is no Lot of Hospitality, but there is a Lot of Travel Abroad. Cf. Firmicus, *Mathesis*, vi. 32, 49.

ties, from the lot to the stars, and in nocturnal [nativites] the other way around; but in the case of [the Lots] of Boldness, Necessity, and Nemesis, in diurnal nativities, from the stars to the lots, but in nocturnal [nativities] from the lots to the stars.

The Diurnal Lots, but in a Nocturnal Nativity, the other way around.[1]

The Lot of Living Abroad from the Sun to Mars.

The Lot of Authority from Mars to the Sun.

The Lot of Windfall from Saturn to Jupiter.

The Lot of Warfare from Mars to Jupiter.

The Lot of Theft from Mercury to Mars.

The Lot of Desire from Jupiter to Venus.

The Lot of Inheritance from Saturn to Venus.

The Lot of Fellowship from Mercury to Venus.

The Lot of Loans from Mercury to Saturn.

The Lot of Victory from Venus to Mars.

The Lot of Action from Mercury to the Moon.

The Lot of Rulership from Jupiter to Venus.

The Lot of Adultery from Venus to Mars.

The Lot of Buying from Venus to Mercury.

The Lot of Parents from the Sun to the Moon.

The Lot of Shipowning from Saturn to Mercury.

The Lot of Slaves from Mars to the Moon.

The Lot of Friends from Mercury to Venus.

---

[1]The list of lots that follows is in one paragraph in the Greek, but I have chosen to present them as individual sentences in order to make them easier to read.

The Lot of Death from Saturn to the Moon.

The Lot of Real Estate from Saturn to Mercury.

The Lot of the Matter at Hand from Jupiter to Mars.

The Lot of Skill from Mars to the Moon.

The Lot of Injury from Mars to Saturn.

The Lot of Livelihood from Venus to Saturn.

The Lot of Life from the Moon to Venus.

The Lot of the Basis from Venus to Mercury.

The Lot of Enemies from Saturn to Mars.

The Lot of Dignity from the Sun to Mars.

The Lot of the Fatherland from Saturn to Mercury.

The Lot of Judgment from Saturn to Jupiter.

The Lot of Leaving Home from Saturn to Mars.

The Lot of Anxiety from Saturn to the Sun.

The Lot of Grief from Saturn to Mars.

The Lot of Action from Jupiter to Venus.

Otherwise, the Lots more Nicely [Set Forth].[1]

The Lot of Livelihood from the Sun to the ASC.

The Lot of Fellowship from Jupiter to Venus.

The Lot of Slaves from Mercury to the Moon.

The Lot of Life from Jupiter to Saturn.

The Lot of Selling from the Sun to Jupiter.

The Lot of Farming from Saturn to Venus.

The Lot of Friends from Jupiter to Venus.

---

[1]Note that in some cases the planets are different from those given for the Lots in the previous section or even earlier in this same section.

The Lot of Honor from Jupiter to Venus.

The Lot of the Will[1] from Mercury to Saturn.

The Lot of Wealth from Jupiter to the Sun.

The Lot of Robustness from the Sun to the MC.

The Lot of Praise from the 2nd part to the Moon's setting.[2]

The Lot of Enemies from Saturn to Mars.

The Lot of Landed Property from Venus to Saturn.

The Lot of Buying from Mars to Venus.

The Lot of Selling from Venus to Mars.

The Lot of Hatred from Mars to Saturn.

The Lot of the Will from Saturn to Jupiter.

The Lot of Fellowship from Mercury to Jupiter.

The Lot of Waters from Venus to Saturn.

The Lot of the Home from Saturn to the Moon.

The Lot of the Tomb from the Moon to Saturn.

The Lot of the Informer from Mercury to Venus.

The Lot of Destruction from Mars to Mercury.

The Lot of Thieves from Mercury to Mars.

The Lot of the Debtor from Saturn to Mercury.

The Lot of the Nativity from the Sun to the 19th degree of Aries.[3]

The Lot of Fortune from the Sun to the Moon.

The Lot of the Daemon from the Moon to the Sun.

---

[1] A legal document for the disposition of the property of a deceased person.

[2] The text is corrupt here, and the â family of MSS omits this sentence.

[3] MS **A** has 'the Lot <[of the] Exaltation> of the Nativity', which is probably correct.

The Lot of Love from the [Lot of the] Daemon to Mercury.[1]

The Lot of Necessity from Mercury to [the Lot of] Fortune.

The Lot of Victory from [the Lot of the] Daemon to Jupiter.

The Lot of Boldness from Mars to [the Lot of] Fortune.

The Lot of Nemesis from Saturn to [the Lot of] Fortune.

The Lot of the Father from the Sun to Saturn.

The Lot of the Mother from Venus to the Moon.

The Lot of Brothers from Saturn to Jupiter.

The Lot of Children from Jupiter to Saturn.

The Lot of Men's Marriages from Saturn to Venus.

The Lot of Women's Marriages from Venus to Saturn (also by night).

The Lot of the Harmful House from Saturn to Mars.[2]

The Lot of the Anaereta from the Ruler of the ASC to the Moon (also by night).

The Lot of Death from the Moon to the Eighth House and the Distance cast from Saturn (also by night).

And these lots are not included in the *Panaretos*, which the Thrice-Great Hermes set forth. For in it he only gave the seven lots, I mean the [Lots] of the Daemon and of Fortune and Necessity and Love and Boldness and Victory and Nemesis. And the very learned Paul added only [the Lots of the] Father and Mother and of Marriage and Children and Brothers.

---

[1]Not Mercury, but rather Venus, perhaps a typographical error in the Greek text.

[2]Cf. Vettius Valens, *Anthology*, v. 1. Wherever this Lot falls, it indicates a place in the nativity that is a potential source of fears and dangers. Since the ancient astrologers used the Sign-House system of celestial houses, this Lot indicates both a sign and a house, which may be dangerous. If it is a bad house, such as the 8th or the 12th, or if the lot receives conjunctions or bad aspects from the malefics, it is an evil indication.

And we have added all the others, having found them in [the books] of other old [authors] in order to bring to an end the topic of Lots. For the consideration of these helps us very much. For in every matter that is taken in hand, whether absence from home, or skill, or friends, or marriage, or anything else of whatever sort you wish, to know the outcome, either useful or useless, go into the list of Lots. And you will look for how the Lot of the matter in hand happens to fall, from which star to which star by day and to which star by night, and you will reckon according to the stated method, and you will find what sort of end the matter will come to. For if that Lot falls into [the place of the] Lot of the Daemon or into [that of] the Lot of Fortune or of Necessity or into the degree, in which the most recent new Moon or full Moon has occurred, or in the sign in which there is a benefic star, or in an angle, all good things will be in that matter, and there will be much success. But if it falls in either a cadent [house] or in where a malefic star is, or somehow the Lot of the matter falls into an evil place, the implementation of it will be useless, and this is the utility of these Lots.

And naturally the first seven Lots, the general ones, I mean those of the seven stars, the divine Hermes called by such names, naming the one of the Moon "Fortune," and the one of the Sun "Daemon," and the next ones, since also by nature the Moon established Fortune, and the Sun Daemon, and Venus Love, and the [star] of Mercury Necessity, and the [star] of Mars Boldness, and the [star] of Jupiter Victory, and the [star] of Saturn Nemesis.

And the ASC of these governs up to the middle, being established as the basis of the whole arrangement, since all the Lots are cast from it, and since the native first draws life from it. And similarly too, every action has its beginning from it; and the [Lot of] Fortune signifies all the things of the body and the actions according to the livelihood, and it was also established to be indicative of property and praise and precedence; but the [Lot of the] Daemon happens to be the ruler of the soul and of habits and understanding and of all sovereignty, and sometimes it also works jointly in the matter of action.

And [the Lot] of Love signifies longings and desires that arise according to the sect, and it was also established as the author of friendship and joy; but the [Lot of] Necessity makes anxieties and subordinations and fights and wars, also enmities and hatreds and condemnations and all the other violent things that happen to men. The [Lot of] Boldness was established as the cause of courage and plots and strength and all acts of villainy. And the [Lot of] Victory was established as the cause of faith and good hope and contest and all association, but also of attack and success. And [the Lot of] Nemesis was established as the cause of spirits of the earth and of those things that were hidden of proof as well as of weakness and flight and destruction and grief and the maker of death.

And the Basis is the ASC, and it was established [to be] the cause of life and breath, since at the time of birth all that which is generated draws forth from the air the vital breath at the moment of the water clock[1] appointed at birth, which is indicative of all things.

In one copy the Lots were found written in this order:

These are the Diurnal Lots.

The Lot of Living Abroad from the Sun to Mars.

The Lot of Wealth from Jupiter to the Sun.[2]

The Lot of Authority from Saturn to Jupiter.

The Lot of Theft from Mercury to Mars.

The Lot of Inheritance from Saturn to Venus

---

[1]That is, at the moment of birth as determined by reference to a clock—in this case, a water clock.
[2]Here and for the succeding Lots I have supplied the words 'The Lot', which are omitted in the Greek text.

The Lot of Loans from Mercury to Saturn.

The Lot of Action from Mercury to the Moon.

The Lot of Adultery from Venus to Mars.

The Lot of the Parents from the Sun to the Moon.

The Lot of Slaves from Mars to the Moon.

The Lot of Death from Saturn to the Moon.

The Lot of Business from Jupiter to Saturn.

The Lot of Injury from Mars to Saturn.

The Lot of Life from the Lot of Fortune to Venus, or

> from Jupiter to Saturn, or
>
> from Venus to Saturn, or
>
> from Venus to Mercury.

The Lot of Enemies from the Sun to Mars.

The Lot of the Fatherland from Saturn to Jupiter.

The Lot of Love from Saturn to Mars.

The Lot of Anxiety from Saturn to Mars.

The Lot of Action from the Sun to Jupiter.

The Lot of Business from Jupiter to Saturn.

The Lot of Forbearance from Saturn to the Sun.

The Lot of Landed Property from Mars to Venus.

The Lot of Farming from Saturn to Venus.

The Lot of the Will from Mercury to Jupiter.

The Lot of Authority from Mars to the Sun.

The Lot of Warfare from Mars to Jupiter.

The Lot of Desire from Jupiter to Venus.

The Lot of Fellowship from Mercury to Venus, or[1]
  from Jupiter to Venus.

The Lot of Victory from Venus to Mars.

The Lot of Rulership and Honor from Jupiter to Venus.

The Lot of Buying from Venus to Mercury.

The Lot of Shipowning from Saturn to Jupiter.

The Lot of Friends from the Moon to Mercury, or
  from Jupiter to Venus.

The Lot of Real Estate from Saturn to Mercury.

The Lot of Skill from Mars to Venus.

The Lot of Livelihood from Venus to the Moon, or
  [from Venus] to Saturn.

The Lot of the Basis from [the Lot of] Fortune to [the Lot of
the] Daemon, or
  from Venus to Mercury.

The Lot of Dignity from Jupiter to the Sun, or
  from the Sun to Mars.

The Lot of Judgments from Saturn to Mercury, or
  [from Saturn] to Mars.

Otherwise, the Lots more Nicely [Set Forth].

The Lot of Livelihood from the Sun to the ASC.

The Lot of Fellowship from Jupiter to Venus.

The Lot of Slaves from Mercury to the Moon.

The Lot of Life from Jupiter to Saturn.

The Lot of Action from the Sun to Jupiter.

---

[1]Following this the **â** family of MSS adds 'or' and following that the MSS
have 'from Jupiter to Venus'. The editor of the Greek text deletes 'or',
but I think it should be retained.

The Lot of Farming from Saturn to Venus.

The Lot of Friends from Jupiter to Venus.

The Lot of Honor from Jupiter to Venus.

The Lot of the Will from Mercury to Jupiter.

The Lot of Wealth from Jupiter to the Sun.

The Lot of Robustness from the Sun to the MC.

The Lot of Praise from the second part [house?] to the Moon.[1]

The Lot of Enemies from Saturn to Mars.

The Lot of Landed Property from Venus to Mars.

The Lot of Buying from Mars to Venus.

The Lot of Selling from the Sun to Mars.

[The following six Lots are from an example list of planetary positions.]

The Lot of Fortune in 17 Capricorn with the Sun trining Mercury and Venus;

The Lot of the Daemon in 22 Gemini with Jupiter sextiling the Sun, squaring . . .;

The Lot of Victory in 21 Aries with the Sun trining . . .;

The Lot of Love in 12 Gemini with Mercury squaring Venus;

The Lot of Marriage in /// squaring Mars;

The Lot of Living Abroad in 13 Gemini with Venus and Saturn sextiling Mars.

[the list of Lots resumes]

The Lot of the Kingdom from the Sun to the Moon and an equal amount from the MC.

---

[1]Here the MSS disagree: **L** has Moon D[SC?], **A** has DSC Moon, the **â** family of MSS has DSC.

The Lot of Exaltation in a diurnal nativity from the Sun to its exaltation, i.e. the 19th of Aries, and an equal amount from the ASC; but by night from the Moon to its exaltation, i.e. the 3rd of Scorpio, and an equal amount from the ASC.

The Lot of Turning About from the Sun to the Moon and an equal amount from Leo.

The Lot of the Other Turning About from the Moon to the Sun and an equal amount from Cancer. But the rulers of these Lots must be observed. For Mars being and falling within the three-sign area is the cause of bloodshed and captivity.

All the Lots of the Ancients.[1]

The Lot of Fortune from the Sun to the Moon by day, but by night from the Moon to the Sun, and I apportion [their interval] from the ASC.

The Lot of the Daemon from the Moon to the Sun by day, but by night the reverse, and an equal amount from the ASC.

The Lot of Basis by day from Fortune to Daemon, but by night the reverse, and an equal amount from the ASC.

The Lot of Desire from the Daemon to Venus by day, but by night the reverse, and an equal amount from the ASC.

The Lot of Necessity by day from Mercury to Fortune, but by night the reverse, and an equal amount from the ASC.

The Lot of Boldness by day from Mars to Fortune, but by night the reverse. The Lot of Victory by day from Daemon to Jupiter, but by night the reverse.

The Lot of Nemesis by day from Saturn to Fortune, but by night the reverse.

---

[1]This section of Chapter 22 is at the end of the chapter and is found only in the 10th century MS **L**, which is the oldest of all the MSS of the *Commentary*.

The Lot of Action by day from Mercury to Mars, but by night the reverse.

The Lot of the Father by day from Mercury to Saturn,[1] but by night the reverse.

The Lot of Military Service by day from Mars to Jupiter, by night the reverse.

The Lot of Military Service[2] by day from Saturn to the Moon, by night the reverse.

The Lot of Livelihood from the ruler of the second house to the second house itself, and cast an equal amount from the ASC both by day and by night.

The Lot of the Mother by day from Venus to the Moon, by night the reverse.

The Lot of Marriage of a Man by day from Saturn to Venus, by night the reverse.

The Lot of the Marriage of a Woman by day from Venus to Saturn, by night the reverse.

The Lot of Life by day from the Moon to Venus, by night the reverse.[3]

The Lot of Finding by day from Venus to Mercury, by night the reverse.

The Lot of Inheritance by day from Jupiter to Mercury, by night the reverse.

The lot of Technical Skill by day from Mars to the Moon, by night the reverse.

The Lot of Livelihood by day from Venus to Saturn, by night the reverse.

---

[1]This should read ". . . from the Sun to Saturn . . ."
[2]*Epistrateias* presumably = *strateias*; both then mean 'military service'.
[3]In the margin of MS **L** (10th cent.) in a much more recent hand, "The Lot of Life from Jupiter to Saturn by day."

The Lot of Children by day from Jupiter to Saturn, by night the reverse.

The Lot of Female Children by day from the Moon to Venus, by night the reverse.[1]

The Lot of Friends by day from the Moon to Mercury, by night the reverse.

The Lot of Slaves by day from Venus[2] to the Moon, by night the reverse.

The Lot of Death by day and by night from Saturn to the Moon, and an equal amount [from the ASC].

The Lot of Death by day from the Moon to Saturn, by night the reverse.

The Lot of Death from the Moon to the 8th sign, and give the distribution from Saturn by day and by night.

The Lot of Injury from Saturn to Mars and cast it from Mercury by day, but by night from Mars to Saturn and cast it from Mercury.

The Lot of Wealth by day from Saturn to the Sun, by night the reverse.

The Lot of Conception by day from the Sun to Mars, by night the reverse.

The Lot of Dreams by day from Saturn to Mercury, by night the reverse.

The Lot of Justice by day from Mercury to Saturn, by night the reverse.

The Lot of Jealousy by day from Mars to Saturn, by night the reverse.

---

[1] In the margin of MS L in a more recent hand, "The Lot of Male Children from the Moon to Jupiter."
[2] In MS L corrected by a more recent hand to Mercury.

The Lot of Loss by day from Mars to Saturn, by night the reverse. The Lot of the Sale by day from Mercury to the Moon, by night the reverse.

The Lot of the Fatherland by day from the Sun to Mars, by night the reverse.

The Lot of Foreign by day from the Sun to Mars, by night the reverse.[1] The Lot of Foreign from the ruler of the 9th house to the 9th house and an equal amount from the ASC by day and by night.

The Lot of the Harmful House by day from Saturn to Mars and an equal amount from Mercury, by night the vice-versa.

The same lot is also said to be that of the Hurtful of the Anaeretic Star from the ruler of the ASC to the Moon and an equal amount from the ASC, but by night vice-versa.

The Lot of the Climacteric Year by day from Saturn to the ruler of the previous new Moon or full Moon and an equal amount from the ASC.

The Lot of the Marriage of a Man according to Valens from the Sun to Venus, but of a Woman from the Moon to Mars, by day and by night.

The Lot of Adultery, by the opposite of [the Lot of] Marriage, from the Sun to the Moon and an equal amount from the ASC by day and by night.

And this indication is in the fourth chapter of the second book of Dorotheus.

The Lot of the Exaltation of the Nativity by day from the Sun to its exaltation [degree].

The Lot of Enemies from Saturn to Mercury.

The Lot of Injury by day and by night from Saturn to Mars.

---

[1]This and the preceding lot should not have the same formula. One of them is probably reversed.

The Lot of Land by day and by night from Venus to Saturn.

The Lot of the Ruler by day and by night from Venus to the Sun.

The Lot of Sickness by day from Saturn to Mercury.

The Lot of Absence from Home by day from Mercury to Mars.

The Lot of Military Service by day from Mercury to Mars.

The Lot of the Lender by day and by night from Saturn to Mercury.

The Lot of Sailing, taking [the interval] by day from Saturn to the degrees of Cancer and distributing it from the ASC, but by night vice-versa.

The Lot of Manumission from Mercury to the Sun.

The Lot of the Lady Friend of a Man by day from the Moon to Jupiter.

The Lot of the Man Friend of a Woman from Jupiter to the Moon.

The Lot of the Man Friend of a Man by day from Venus to Jupiter.

The Lot of Brothers by day and by night from Saturn to Jupiter.

But in all of the lots, you must take the degrees of the ASC and distribute from them. All the aforementioned lots are distributed from the ASC without this having been [specifically] mentioned.

[Translator's Note. If I have counted them correctly, there are 98 different lots mentioned in these lists.]

Index of the Lots

Absence from Home 128,137

Action 124,125,130,131,134

Adultery 124,130,136

Anaereta 136

Anxiety 125,130

Authority 124,129,130

Basis 43,45,125,131,133

Boldness 42,43,122,127,129,133

Brothers 45,122,123,127,137

Business 123,130

Buying 124,126,131,132

Children 45,60,102,106,107,122,123,127,135

Climacteric Year 136

Conception 135

Daemon 39,41,42,43,44,46,81,102,107,115,117,119,121,122,
123,126,127,128,131,132,133

Death 125,127,130,135

Debtor 126

Desire 124,130,133

Destruction 126

Dignity 125,131

Dreams 135

Enemies 125,126,130,132,136

Exaltation 45,133,136

Exaltation of Nativity 133

Farming 125,130,132

Father 44,45,102,123,127,134

Fatherland 125,130,136

Fellowship 124,125,126,131

Female Children 135

Finding 134

Forbearance 130

Foreign 136

Fortune 39,41,42,43,44,46,62,63,76,81,85,102,114,116,117,119,
120,121,122,123,126,127,128,130,131,132,133

Friends 124,125,131,132

Grief 125

Harmful House 127,136

Hatred 126

Home 126

Honor 126,132

Hurtful 136

Informer 126

Inheritance 124,129,134

Injury 45,125,130,135,136

Jealousy 135

Judgment 125

Judgments 131

Justice 135

Kingdom 132

Lady Friend of a Man 137

Land 137

Landed Property 126,130,132

Leaving Home 125

Lender 137

Life 125,130,131,134

Livelihood 125,131,134

Living Abroad 124,129,132

Loans 124,130

Loss 136

Love 42,43,44,122,123,127,129,130,132

Male Children 135n.1

Man Friend of a Man 137

Man Friend of a Woman 137

Manumission 137

Marriage of Men 45,123,127,134,136

Marriage of Women 127,134

Matter at Hand 125

Military Service 134,137

Mother 45,122,123,127,134

Nativity 126

Necessity 39,42,43,122,123,127,128,129,133

Nemesis 122,127,129,133

Other Turning About 133

Parents 124,130

Praise 126,132

Real Estate 1254,131

Robustness 126,132

Ruler 137

Rulership 124

Rulership and Honor 131

Sailing 137

Sale 136

Selling 125,126,132

Shipowning 124,131

Sickness 137

Skill 125,131

Slaves 124,125,130,131,135

Technical Skill 134

Theft 124,129

Thieves 126

Tomb 126

Travel Abroad 123

Turning About 133

Victory 42,43,122,123,124,127,129,131,132,133

Warfare 124,130

Waters 126

Wealth 126,129,132,135

Will 71,74,75

Will (Testament) 71

Windfall 70

[Note: these are references to the *formula* for a Lot,
not to an incidental mention of it.]

Appendix II

The Horoscope of Cronamon

In Chapters 23 and 31 Paul gives elements of a horoscope as examples of the topic under discussion. These are:

	from Chapter 23:	from Chapter 31:
Sun	28 Pisces	Ascendant in Leo
Moon	28 Aquarius	Mercury in Aries
Ascendant	11 Leo	Jupiter in Gemini
Venus	15 Aquarius	Saturn in Taurus

and we are also told that these elements belong to the horoscope of a native for whom the 26th revolution of his horoscope is to be considered. This chart was overlooked by Boer, when she edited the text (1958), and it was also overlooked by Neugebauer and Van Hoesen, when they compiled *Greek Horoscopes* (published 1959).

From the elements shown above it is easy to determine that the date of the horoscope was 19 March 353 at about the 8th hour of the day (about 2 PM), and the place was presumably Alexandria. We may then compute the planetary positions at that time from modern astronomical elements and compare them with the positions given by Paul.

---

[1]This information was published in the AFA *Journal of Research*, Vol. 5, No. 1 (Autumn 1989): 7-10.

It will also be of interest to calculate the Ptolemaic positions for that same time. In calculating the Ptolemaic positions, I have used my computer program with the Ptolemaic elements as given in his *Syntaxis*. They may, therefore, differ by a few minutes from positions calculated directly from an extension of his tables (or from his *Handy Tables*). To the calculated positions I have added the "Correction" mentioned by Theon of Alexandria to reduce the Ptolemaic positions approximately to positions in the fixed Alexandrian zodiac.[1] For the year 353 the Correction amounts to +1°38'.

Planet	Text	Calculated[2]	Ptolemaic + Correction
Sun	28 Psc	29 Psc 20	29 Psc 13
Moon	28 Aqu	26 Aqu 27	27 Aqu 02
Mercury	Ari	18 Ari 33	19 Ari 23
Venus	15 Aqu	14 Aqu 22	14 Aqu 28
Mars	- - - -	10 Can 48	9 Can 34
Jupiter	Gem	8 Gem 27	9 Gem 01
Saturn	Tau	28 Tau 021	26 Tau 35
Ascendant	11 Leo		

I think it very likely that this is the horoscope of Paul's son Cronamon.

---

[1] For more information on the "Correction," see my paper "The Classical Zodiac" in the *Journal of Research* of the American Federation of Astrologers, Vol. 7, No. 2 (1995): 9-16.
[2] Using a value of Delta T = +1:84. The figures shown differ slightly from those given in my 1989 paper, since there I used a different value of Delta T (+2:33).

COMMENTARY

1. SIGNS THAT SEE EACH OTHER AND THE
COMMANDING AND OBEYING SIGNS.

The pairs of signs given by Paul are the same as those given by Manilius, *Astronomica*, ii.466-519. They hark back to a fixed zodiac in the early days of astrology, in which the equinoctial line ran through the middle of Aries and Libra, and the tropical line ran through the middle of Cancer and Capricorn. Thus, the sign pairs given by Paul were those that were equally distant from the equinoctial signs or the tropical signs. These pairings became established in the earlier astrological literature.

Later, when the fixed zodiac was abandoned in favor of the tropical zodiac, the lines shifted from the middle of the equinoctial and tropical signs to the beginning of those signs. Signs that see each other were then logically on opposite sides of the tropical line, but on the same side of the equinoctial line. Hence, when the Sun was in 15 Taurus the day had the same length as when the Sun was in 15 Leo. Commanding and obeying signs were the other way around—located opposite each other across the equinoctial line, one in the northern hemisphere ("commanding") and the other in the southern hemisphere ("obeying").

A further development of the signs that see each other was the *antiscion*. This was an exact degree that "saw" the original degree. Passing mention is made of "antiscial degrees" by Vettius Valens,[1] but the only extensive account that has come down to us from classical antiquity is in Firmicus, *Mathesis*, ii. 30, who even gives a de-

---

[1]Anthology, iii. 11 and vi. 8.

gree table. Firmicus says that Dorotheus of Sidon gave a clear and detailed account of *antiscia* in the 4th book of his *Pentateuch*. Unfortunately, the original Greek of that work has perished except for some scattered citations in later authors. An examination of Pingree's translation of his edition of an Arabic text, said to have been translated from an earlier Pahlavi translation of Dorotheus, shows that the Arabic version is both incomplete and interpolated. And its fourth book, which consists solely of a single chapter, now contains nothing on the subject of *antiscia*.

Towards the end of the first century B.C., perhaps a generation or two before Manilius, Geminus of Rhodes, *Introduction to the Phenomena*, ii. Sections 27-45, discussed the seeing and hearing signs. He does not use these terms but calls them *syzygiai* 'paired' signs. In Sections 27-32 he sets forth the theory of these paired signs as postulated by the "ancients" (*archaioi*). Then, in Sections 33-45, he states that their theory is completely false, explains why, and gives a revised list in Section 44: Gemini-Cancer, Taurus-Leo, Aries-Virgo, Pisces-Libra, Aquarius-Scorpio, and Capricorn-Sagittarius.

Like Bouché-Leclercq[1] two thousand years later, Geminus does not seem to have realized that the pairings given by the ancients were quite correct for a zodiac that put the summer solstice at 15 degrees of Cancer. So long as horoscopes were calculated from an ephemeris that used that norm, the ancient pairings were correct. But, if horoscopes were calculated from an ephemeris that began the zodiac at the vernal equinox, then they were not correct, and the revised series given by Geminus should logically have been substituted. But the tropical zodiac had not yet come into use among astrologers. In Geminus's day they were using the fixed Alexandrian zodiac, in which the equinoctial and tropical points were at the 8th degree of the cardinal signs, not far from 15°. We can see what the situation was like in the second century A.D. by

---

[1] L'Astrologie Grecque, pp. 159-64.

noting Ptolemy's discussion of these pairings. In his *Tetrabiblos*, i. 15, he explains the ancient theory but he is careful not to name the signs, since, following Hipparchus, he had shifted the cardinal points to the beginning of Aries, Cancer, Libra, and Capricorn, which would logically alter the pairing to agree with that given by Geminus. Thus, he gave tacit approval to the old system.

Vettius Valens has a chapter entitled "Obeying and Seeing Signs" (*Anth.*, i. 8), but, as Housman pointed out (*M. Manilii Astronomicon*, v. 2, p. xviii), it expounds a completely different theory. Valens lived in Alexandria either during or shortly after the lifetime of Ptolemy but shows no awareness of either his astrological or astronomical works.[1] In fact, his horoscopes are calculated in the Alexandrian zodiac, which in his time actually began 4 or 5 degrees before the vernal equinox.[2]

Porphyry, *Introduction*, Chapters 31 and 33,[3] sticks with the pairings defined by the ancients for the (commanding and) obeying signs and the signs that see each other, but in Chapter 32 he gives the new system of commanding and obeying signs under the heading of "signs of equal power," adding that they are only said to be signs that "obey each other" (sic!) or signs that see each other **because of their shadows**. This statement refers to the Greek word *antiskios* 'antiscion', which literally means 'opposite shadow', referring to the fact that in the tropical zodiac the pairs have the same declination (of opposite algebraic sign in the case of the commanding and obeying signs, and of the same algebraic sign in the case of the signs that see each other).

---

[1] This demonstrates that Ptolemy's works were not available to the public in the second century A.D. See my paper "Claudius Ptolemy" in the American Federation of Astrologers *Journal of Research*, Vol. 13 (2010): 121-130.
[2] See my paper "The Classical Zodiac" in the American Federation of Astrologers *Journal of Research*, Vol. 7, No. 2 (1995): 9-16; and also my book, *A History of Horoscopic Astrology* (Tempe, Az.: A.F.A., Inc., 1996; 2nd ed. 2006).
[3] See my translation, Porphyry the Philosopher, *Introduction to the Tetrabiblos* (Tempe, Az.: A.F.A., Inc., 2009).

Taken together, Porphyry's Chapters 31-33 present a confused picture, but not nearly so complicated as that given by Manilius (loc. cit.) or Firmicus (*Mathesis*, viii. 3). Interestingly enough, Porphyry's book was supposed to be an introduction to Ptolemy's *Tetrabiblos*, but, while Ptolemy is straightforward even if old-fashioned, Porphyry confuses the terminology and injects an explanation of the new system which Ptolemy had not mentioned at all.

Hephaestio of Thebes wrote his *Apotelesmatics* in the early years of the fifth century. His Chapters in i. 9 "Commanding and Obeying (Signs)" and i. 10 "(Signs) of Equal Power and that See (Each Other)" are paraphrases of Ptolemy, *Tetrabiblos*, i. 14 and 15.

Rhetorius's *Astrological Compendium*,[1] Chapter 19 "Obeying and Seeing (Signs)" gives the old system in an abbreviated form. It reduces the category of "commanding and obeying signs" to that of "signs that obey each other." In this respect, it follows the terminology of Porphyry's Chapters 31 and 33.

Modern astrologers ignore these sign classifications, but they use an "aspect" called the *parallel* which occurs when two points on the zodiac have the same declination, either both north or one north and the other south. This is a modification of the antiscion. Generally, an "orb" of 1 degree is allowed.

2. CALCULATION OF THE DAY OF THE WEEK FROM THE ALEXANDRIAN DATE.

In Paul's time the people of Alexandria used the Egyptian calendar as reformed by the emperor Augustus but with the era of Diocletian. The Augustan reform nominally dates from 30 B.C. and commemorates the passage of power from the dynasty of the

---

[1] See my translation, Rhetorius the Egyptian, *Astrological Compendium* (Tempe, Az.: A.F.A., Inc., 2009).

Ptolemies to Rome. It added a leap day every four years to keep the Egyptian calendar in synchronism with the newly revised Roman calendar. Once both sets of reforms were established, the Egyptian New Year's Day, 1 Thoth, fell on 29 August in three successive years, followed by a coincidence with 30 August in the Roman year preceding the leap year in the Julian calendar. Unlike the Julian calendar, which extended the month of February by one day, the reformed Egyptian calendar added the leap day as a 366th day of the year in which it occurred.

Since neither the Romans nor the Egyptians had an era that was in common use, dating was usually by years of the emperor. In Egypt an emperor's reign was considered to date from New Year's Day of the year in which he came to power. Diocletian was raised to the purple on 17 November 284; hence, the Egyptian year which had begun on 29 August 284 became the 1st year of Diocletian. However, unlike most other emperors, people continued to use his regnal years even after he abdicated in the 21st year of his reign (1 May 305 = 6 Pachon 21 Diocletian). This evidently satisfied the need for a continuous year count.[1]

The Egyptian calendar consisted of twelve months of thirty days each, whose names were Thoth, Phaophi, Athyr, Choiak, Tybi, Mecheir, Phamenoth, Pharmouthi, Pachon, Payni, Epiphi, and Mesori, followed by 5 additional days (6 in leap year) that were called *epagomenai* 'brought in' or 'intercalated'.[2] Various days were sacred to the Egyptian gods, and others were holidays or named days.

With this information in hand, we may ask ourselves why Paul felt it needful to present an explanation of how to calculate the day of the 7-day week. There were many Christians in Alexandria in

---

[1] See Vettius Valens, *Anthology*, i. 10, for a similar procedure using the years of Augustus.
[2] O. Neugebauer remarked with justification that this was the only sensible calendar ever invented.

his day. They would have had calendars showing the 7-day week. Presumably there were shops where such things could be bought. However, we may assume that knowledge of the 7-day week had not yet become necessary to the pagan population of Alexandria. Of course they would have been aware of its existence, but it evidently did not affect their civil life or daily activities beyond the point of needing to know upon occasion whether a Jewish or Christian merchant might be open for business on a particular day. We must assume then that pagans did not keep calendars handy that showed the 7-day week. Nor did they have handbooks showing the correspondences for years in the past. Therefore, if such information was wanted, it would have to be calculated.

Paul evidently knew that the date 1 Thoth 1 Diocletian (29 August 284) fell on the 6th day of the week, i.e. Friday. To find the number of the day of the week for any subsequent date, it was only necessary to determine the number of days that had elapsed between the two dates, divide by 7, throw out the weeks and keep the left over days, add them to 5, throw out any whole weeks, and there was the answer. His means of doing this is straightforward, making allowance for the ancient lack of zero and for their habit of counting both ends of a sequence.

The common year consisted of 365 days or 52,1 weeks; the leap year had 52,2 weeks. Thus, in the two common years and in leap year itself the day of the week of each numbered day advanced 1 day in the week over the corresponding date in the previous year; but in the year following leap year, it advanced 2 days. Hence, the rule: count the years since Diocletian and add to it 1/4 of the number, ignoring fractions. (This rule takes advantage of the fact that the year 1 Diocletian was the first of the three common years, so that the rule of four for finding leap year is valid just as it is in our calendar.) In practice, Paul simply takes the actual year number and increases it by 1/4. But since he has counted the year he set out from, his result is 1 too high.

Next, a similar calculation must be made within the year to determine the elapsed days since 1 Thoth. The 30 days of each month amount to 4,2 weeks, so the weekday of each numbered day advances 2 days each month. Hence, the rule: count the months since Thoth and multiply by 2, then add the days since the 1st of the month. In practice it is easier to double the month number and add the day of the month for which the weekday is sought. But this produces an additional error of 2 days from the month and 1 day from the day of the month for a total error of 3 days.

Paul disposes of the combined 4-day error neatly. He subtracts it from the weekday number of Friday, i.e. 6, and gets 2. Then he splits his calculation into two parts because the part of the calculation depending on the year is valid for the whole year. So in Chapter 19 he tells us how to calculate a number that is 3 less than the weekday number for 1 Thoth of a particular year. He calls this number "the Days of the Gods," by which he means "the number that is to be used for calculating weekdays." Then in Chapter 20 he tells us how to calculate the augment for the month and day. By adding the two numbers together and excluding whole weeks of 7 days, the weekday number results.

Let us follow his calculation for 20 Mecheir 94 Diocletian (14 February 378). For the year: $2 + 94 + INT(94/4) = 119$; divide by 7, it comes out even, so call the remainder 7.[1] Next, for the month and day: Mecheir is the 6th month, double 6, it equals 12; the number from the year calculation is 7; the day of the month number is 20; add these three numbers, $7 + 12 + 20 = 39$; divide by 7, the remainder is 4; this is the weekday number, and the weekday is Wednesday.

Here is an example for the day of epoch, 1 Thoth 1 Diocletian. For the year: $2 + 1 + INT(1/4) = 3$. For the month and day: $2 + 1 = 3$. Combining the numbers: $3 + 3 = 6$; the day is Friday.

---

[1]The ancients had no zero, so in cyclical numbering they used the maximum number where we would use zero.

A final example. What was the weekday of the date 13 Athyr 1701 Diocletian? For the year: 2 + 1701 + 425 = 2128; divide by 7, it comes out even, so we say the result is 7. For the month and day: Athyr is the 3rd month, twice 3 is 6; the day of the month number is 13; adding all the numbers, 7 + 6 + 13 = 26; divide by 7, the remainder is 5, so the weekday number was Thursday. And in fact it was Thursday 22 November 1984, Thanksgiving Day in the U.S.A..

Paul's method can be expressed by algorithms in the BASIC language as follows. Let Y be the year of Diocletian, G the "days of the gods," M the month number, D the day of the month, and W the day of the week (Sunday = 1). Then we calculate

G = (Y + INT(Y/4) + 2) MOD 7

W = (G + 2*M + D) MOD 7

or, combining the two algorithms

W = (INT(5*Y/4) + 2 + 2*M + D) MOD 7

3. CALCULATION OF THE APPROXIMATE DEGREE OF THE SUN.

One way to calculate the approximate longitude of the Sun on a given day is to calculate the Sun's mean longitude and ignore the solar equation of the center, which can add or subtract a maximum of 2 degrees to the mean longitude. Paul seems to have had this in mind, although we cannot be absolutely sure, since the MSS give two different constant figures and since Paul does not give us a worked example.

In Chapt. 28 his method for the "rough" calculation of the Sun's degree is as follows:

1. "Gather together" the days from 1 Thoth to the day sought.

2. Divide the months from Thoth by 2 and subtract the integer part of the quotient from the result of Step 1.

3. Add the result of Step 2 to 156. If the sum is greater than 360, then subtract 360.

4. Subtract multiples of 30 degrees. The number of multiples + 1 is the number of the sign the Sun is in, and the number of degrees remaining is its degree number.

While this method is fairly simple, two problems arise: (1) MS Y gives 158 degrees for the constant figure, while MS D (and Heliodorus) give 156; and (2) Paul doesn't make it clear (by an example) whether we are to count elapsed days and months from 1 Thoth or whether to count the starting day and month as part of the total. In this instance, I think he intended to count elapsed days, contrary to what he did in calculating the weekday. If so, then his rule expressed as an algorithm is:

$$S = (156 + (M-1)*30 - INT((M-1)/2) + D-1) \bmod 360$$

$$\text{sign number} = INT(S)+1$$

$$\text{degree number} = S - INT(S/30)*30$$

where S is the Sun's degree, M is the month number, and D is the Day number.

If this interpretation of Paul's rules is correct, then for 1 Thoth the approximate longitude of the Sun would be S = 156 + 0 - 0 +0) = 156 or 6 Virgo. Or, if the constant term should be 158, the longitude would be 8 Virgo.

Since Paul was familiar with Ptolemy's *Handy Tables*, we can compare this longitude with mean longitudes from the tables. Paul's rule makes no adjustment for years, so perhaps we should take an average of the solar position on 1 Thoth for four succesive years beginning with the year 377 A.D. From the tables we find for Alexandria Mean Noon:

Julian Date	M S L	T S L	MSL+C	T S L+C
29 Aug 377	156°02′	153°39′	157°21′	154°58′
29 Aug 378	155°47′	153°24′	157°06′	154°43′
30 Aug 379	156°32′	154°09′	157°50′	155°26′
29 Aug 380	156°17′	153°54′	157°34′	155°11′

where MSL is Mean Solar Longitude, TSL is True Solar Longitude, MSL+C is Mean Solar Longitude + the "Correction," and TSL+C is the True Solar Longitude + the "Correction." The "Correction" is the quantity Theon of Alexandria (in his edition of the *Handy Tables*) tells us how to calculate. It is the correction to be added to positions derived from Ptolemy's tables to reduce them to the zodiac used by the early Alexandrian astrologers. It ranges from +1°19′ in 377 to +1°16′ in 380.

It seems to me that what Paul did was to take the tabular MSL for 1 Thoth, whose average value was 156°10′, and adopt it for his constant (156). This was the appropriate thing to do because the maximum value of the Equation of the Center in Ptolemy's tables was 2°23′. Around 1 Thoth the Equation was negative (as in the table above), and 6 months later around 4 Phamenoth it would have been positive. On this date in the year 378 (28 February) MSL = 336°24′ and TSL = 338°47′. The algorithm above gives S = 156 + 180 - 3 + 3 = 336. The difference TSL - MSL is - 2°23′ on 1 Thoth and + 2°47′. Thus, Paul's rule yields a solar longitude that is approximately equal to the Ptolemaic mean longitude of the Sun and has a maximum deviation from the Ptolemaic true longitude of about 3°.

The only solar longitude that Paul gives explicitly is for the date 23 Phamenoth. The solar longitude is given as 28 Pisces. Using the algorithm above, we find S = 156 + 180 - 3 + 22 = 355 or 25 Pisces. This is 3° less than the given longitude. However, it is possible that Paul did not use the solar method of Chapter 28, which he characterizes as "rough," but instead used Ptolemy's tables. If so, the MSL given by those tables would have been 355°08' and the TSL 27°44' Pisces or very nearly 28° Pisces.

Heliodorus, Chapter 27, To Know the Degree of the Sun and the Degree of the ASC.

". . . . For example, as on the present day, hour and month, I mean in fact the 28th of Payni, I want to know where is the Sun, in which [degree] thus. I reckon the [days] from Thoth, the first month, up to the present hour (day), which is 28 Payni. They are months, 298 days,[1] since the 28 of the 10th month are to be added. To these I add generally 156, it makes 454. From these I take away the half of the aforesaid 10 months. The remainder comes to 449. Then I take away a circle, i.e. 360. The remainder comes to 89. I cast these 89 from Aries, by 30's: 30 to Aries, 30 to Taurus; the remainder comes to 29 Gemini. And this is the method by which we more readily find the Sun, in which sign and in which degree it is. . . ."

Earlier in his book (Chapter 18) Heliodorus calculated the day of the week for 20 Payni 280 Diocletian, which is equivalent to 14 June 564, so probably the example in Chapter 27 was set down 8 days later on 28 Payni 280 Diocletian or 22 June 564.[2]

Note that Heliodorus takes the difference of the months between 1 Thoth and 28 Payni but does not take the difference of the days.

---

[1]The printed text has *hōrai* 'hours', which is wrong, but a marginal note in MS **b** has correctly *hēmerai* 'days'.
[2]And in fact if we calculate the Sun's position from Ptolemy's tables, we find that the Sun's longitude was 89°.

4. RISING TIMES FROM THE
ARITHMETICAL PROGRESSION.

Paul finds the accumulated rising time of 15 Leo by simply taking the accumulated rising time of the sign Cancer (106 2/3 equinoctial times) plus 1/2 of the individual rising time of the sign Leo
(35 equinoctial times) or 106 2/3 + 1/2 (35) = 106 2/3 + 17 1/2 =
124 1/6. This procedure would have seemed logical to most classical astrologers. However, it is not strictly correct.

In the latitude of Alexandria, the arithmetical progression
(called "Type A" by science historians) gives the following rising
times in degrees for the individual signs:

Aries	21 2/3	Pisces
Taurus	25	Aquarius
Gemini	28 1/3	Capricorn
Cancer	31 2/3	Sagittarius
Leo	35	Scorpio
Virgo	38 1/3	Libra

Those who have a flair for mathematics can see that it is unrea-
sonable to suppose that the first degree of a sign rises at the same
rate as the last degree. And in fact it does not. The first degree of
each sign in the first quadrant of the zodiac rises more rapidly than
the second degree, the second degree rises more rapidly than the
third degree, and so on. Otherwise we would have the situation
that the last degree of Aries rises in 13/18 of a degree, while the adjacent degree, the first degree of Taurus, rises in 15/18. However,
the arithmetical progression by signs makes no allowance for this,
and seems to imply that every degree of Aries rises in 13/18, every
degree of Taurus in 15/18, every degree of Gemini in 17/18, etc.

To show that this is not correct even for the arithmetical rising
times, we can construct a series of rising times for each 15° seg-
ment of the zodiac. It would look like this:

Aries 1	10 5/12		Pisces 2
Aries 2	11 3/12		Pisces 1
Taurus 1	12 1/12		Aquarius 2
Taurus 2	12 11/12		Aquarius 1
Gemini 1	13 9/12	Capricorn 2	
Gemini 2	14 7/12	Capricorn 1	
Cancer 1	15 5/12	Sagittarius 2	
Cancer 2	16 3/12	Sagittarius 1	
Leo 1	17 1/12	Scorpio 2	
Leo 2	17 11/12	Scorpio 1	
Virgo 1	18 9/12	Libra 2	
Virgo 2	19 7/12	Libra 1	

where Aries 1 = 1-15 Aries, Aries 2 = 15-30 Aries, and similarly for the other signs.

Now, if we add all the individual rising times through Leo 1, we get 123 9/12 equinoctial times for the cumulative total. But Paul got 124 1/6. Hence, his error was 3/12 + 1/6 = 5/12 of an equinoctial time (degree) or 0°25′. This error is relatively small compared to the other errors inherent in his method and to the error incurred by using arithmetical rising times rather than trigonometric rising times.

5. THE THEORY OF THE ARITHMETIC RISING TIMES.

The arithmetic rising times used by the majority of the classical Greek astrologers go back to an exposition of the method by the Alexandrian mathematician Hypsicles (2nd century B.C.) in his book *Anaphorikos* 'Ascension'. Hypsicles lived before the invention of spherical trigonometry, so his method is purely arithmetic. It is in fact based upon a method developed by Babylonian astronomers.

Through the use of the water clock the Babylonians were able to measure the length of the day at the summer solstice and the winter solstice. They noted that the length of the day was shortest at the winter solstice and steadily increased until it reached its maximum at the summer solstice. Also, at the equinoxes, the length of the day was equal to the length of the night. These observations suggested that a numerical progression could be devised to give the length of the day at intermediate times. And, since it was of interest to know when a particular sign would rise, they arranged their progression to give the rising times of the individual signs.

Modern researchers, notably the late O. Neugebauer, have analyzed Hypsicles's arithmetical theory. The following account is based on Neugebauer's discussion in his book *A History of Ancient Mathematical Astronomy* (New York Heidelberg Berlin: Springer Verlag, 1975. 3 vols.).

Notation:

M length of the longest day in equinoctial hours or equinoctial times (degrees)

m length of the shortest day in equinoctial hours or equinocial times (degrees)

R_n rising time in degrees of the sign n (Aries = 1, Taurus = 2, etc.)

A_n rising time in degrees of an individual degree (1 Aries = 1, 2 Aries= 2, etc.)

D difference in rising times of a pair of signs (e.g. Aries and Taurus)

d difference in rising times of a pair of degrees (e.g. 5 Taurus and 6 Taurus)

It was observed that the rising times of the last six signs are the same as the rising times of the first six signs but in reversed order. That is, Aries and Pisces have the same rising time, Taurus and Aquarius have the same rising time, etc. Hence $R_1 = R_{12}$, $R_2 = R_{11}$, etc.

Now plainly the longest day will occur when the Sun is at the beginning of Cancer; hence, if we add the rising times of the 6 signs Cancer through Sagittarius, their sum will equal the length of the longest day, or

$$M = R_4 + R_5 + R_6 + R_7 + R_8 + R_9$$

but $R_4 = R_9$, $R_5 = R_8$, $R_6 = R_7$, so we can write

$$M = 2(R_4 + R_5 + R_6)$$

and similarly m $= 2(R_1 + R_2 + R_3)$

and if we take R_1 , the rising time of Aries, as a fundamental quantity, then the rising times of the signs Aries, Taurus, Gemini, etc., can be expressed as R_1 , $(R_1 + D)$, $(R_1 + 2D)$, etc., where D is the constant difference in the rising signs. And substituting these equivalents into the preceding equation, we can write

$$m = 6(R_1 + D)$$
$$M = 6(R_4 + D)$$

but $R_4 = R_1 + 3D$, so

$$M = 6(R_1 + 4D)$$

now if we subtract the equation for m from the equation for M, we have

$$M - m = 24D - 6D = 18D$$

hence

$$D = (M - m)/18$$

and, having found D, we can now find R_1 from

$$R_1 = m/6 - D$$

Furthermore, we can derive an equation for the cumulative rising time of a single degree.

$$d = D/900$$
$$A_1 = R_1 /15 - 29d$$
$$CRT (A_n) = nA_1 + n(n - 1)d/2$$

Note that this last equation determines the sum of the rising times of the individual degrees from n = 1 to n = k, where k is the degree measured from 0 Aries (not from the beginning of each sign).

We now have all the equations to determine the rising times of the signs and degrees for any particular place as a function of the length of the longest and shortest days in that latitude. The ancients determined that at Alexandria the longest day was 14 hours and the shortest day was 10 hours. So we calculate

$$D = (M - m)/18 = (14 - 10)/18 = 4/18 \text{ hours}$$

but 1 hour equals 15 degrees, so 4/18 hours = 3°20′

or we can express M and m in degrees (210° and 150° respectively), and we will have

$$D = (M - m)/18 = (210° - 150°)/18 = 60°/18 = 3°20′$$

Next we find R_1 from

$$R_1 = m/6 - D = 150°/6 - 3°20′ = 25° - 3°20′ = 21°40′$$

This is the rising time of Aries in degrees. To find the rising time of Taurus and the rest of the signs, we only need to add 3°20′ successively to each rising time. And we have the table

Aries	21°40′	Pisces
Taurus	25°00′	Aquarius
Gemini	28°20′	Capricorn
Cancer	31°40′	Sagittarius
Leo	35°00′	Scorpio
Virgo	38°20′	Libra

If we want to calculate the cumulative rising time of a particular degree, we can use the equation derived above. For example, calculate the cumulative rising time of 15 Leo, which Paul used in his example:

$$d = D/900 = 3°20′ /900 = 1/270 = 0.0037\ 0370\ 37°$$

$$A_1 = 1/2(R_1 /15 - 29\ (0.0037\ 03703)) =\ 0.6685\ 18518$$

$$CRT = 135\ (0.6685\ 18518° +\ (134)\ (0.0037\ 0370\ 37°)/2) = 123.75 = 123°45′$$

which is the same value we derived above by a different means.

To calculate a table of rising times for another clime (latitude), we only need to know the length of the longest day or the shortest day ($M + m = 24$ hours, so $M = 12 - m$), and then we can repeat the calculation. Hypsicles only made the calculation for Alexandria, but it is easy to extend the method to other climes. And in fact Vettius Valens explains an easier way to make the calculations in *Anthology* i. 6. His rules are very simple:

1. Multiply the hours of the longest day by 15 to convert them to degrees. Take 1/6 of the degrees—that gives you the rising time of Leo or R_5.

2. Subtract the rising time of Leo from 60° to obtain the rising time of Aquarius or R_{11}. Then subtract the rising time of Aquarius from the rising time of Leo and divide the difference by 3. This gives you the incremental difference D.

3. Subtract the difference D successively from R_5 to get the rising times of the earlier signs, and add the difference D to R_5 to get the rising time of Virgo.

This method is so easy that with a little practice you can do it in your head. All you need to know is the Clime, i.e. the length of the longest day in equinoctial hours. Here is an example for the Clime in which the longest day is 14 hours.

1. 14 x 15° = 210°   210°/6 = 35°   That is the rising time of Leo.

2. The rising time of Aquarius is 60° - 35° = 25°   (35° - 25°) /3 = 10°/3 = 3°20' , which is D.

3. Subtract and add D successively to obtain the other signs.

Vettius Valens or his source took advantage of the fact that R_5, the rising time of Leo, is the average value of R_4, R_5, and R_6. Consequently, the equation $M = 2(R_4 + R_5 + R_6)$ can be written $M = 6R_5$, whence $R_5 = M/6$. And $R_5 = R_1 + 4D$, while $R_{11} = R_2 = R_1 + D$; therefore, $R_5 - R_{11} = (R_1 + 4D) - (R_1 + D) = 3D$, so $D = (R_5 - R_{11})/3$.

But a much simpler way to determine the rising times is this:

D = 2 arc cos (–tan ε tan ö)

Rising time of Aries = 80° – 5D/18

Interval = abs (D/9 – 20°)

Where D = maximum length of the day in degrees of sidereal time

ε = the Obliquity of the Ecliptic

ö = the geographic latitude of the place

Valens also explains how to calculate the rising times for climes more northerly than Alexandria, which he designates as Clime 1. To construct the rising time table for the second clime, you simply add 4° to the length of the longest day (expressed in degrees) of the preceding clime. Thus, for Clime 1 M = 210°, so for Clime 2 M = 214°, for Clime 3 M = 218°, and so on up to Clime 7, where M = 234°. Valens begins his series of climes with Alexandria as No. 1, which was evidently the original astrological scheme.

Ptolemy (*Syntaxis* ii. 9) gives a more extensive set of 11 tables, calculated trigonometrically, at half hour intervals from M = 12 hours to M = 17 hours, of which Lower Egypt (which included Alexandria) was the 5th. These tables range from 0° N to 54° N. However, in ii. 13 he gives another set of 7 tables at half hour intervals, ranging from M = 13 to M = 16, corresponding to latitudes from about 16 1/2 to 48 1/2 N; and of these, Lower Egypt (including Alexandria) is the third clime. Paul follows that numbering, twice in Chapter 2 expressly identifying Alexandria as lying in Clime 3. Ptolemy's tables were of course much more accurate than those constructed by the arithmetical method; however, his tables do not seem to have become available until around 300 A.D., so for 500 years the astrologers of the classical period had to make do with the older and less accurate figures.[1]

The working astrologer in antiquity probably kept a document with the rising times for the different climes and perhaps also a list

[1]And these arithmetic rising times passed to the Hindus, when they learned astronomy and astrology from Greek books in the second century A.D. They are found, for example, in Varahamihira's *Brihat Jataka*, Chapter 1, Sloka 19, where the "measures of the first six signs" are stated to be 20, 24, 28, 32, 36, and 40; nothing is said about climes or rising times, so it appears that Varahamihira did not recognize what they were. These are actually rising times for Babylon, where the ratio between the longest day and the shortest day is 3:2; they were certainly not appropriate for the lower latitude of India. These same figures appear in Babylonian texts and also in Manilius, *Astronomica*, iii. 275 ff (where they are given in "stades" or half-degrees), and in Firmicus, *Mathesis*, ii. 16.

of cities or countries and their climes. These took the place of our modern Tables of Houses and astrological gazeteers. (Most ancient astrologers used the Sign-House system of houses, so really only a table of Ascendants was needed, for, if the astronomical MC degree was wanted, it could be calculated from the ASC by the method Paul explains.)

How accurately could an astrologer determine the ASC with these tools?

First, we must be aware that the typical astrologer was given a birth time that at best had an average error of plus or minus 30 minutes of time and might very well be one hour or more in error. By day, time was reckoned by sundials, often rather small (there were portable sundials that could be carried about like a modern pocket watch). And these were usually graduated in hours, so that a time would be observed as "at the 3rd hour" if the shadow fell on that line or "between the 3rd and the 4th hour" if it fell half way between the 3rd and 4th hour lines. But a worse problem was caused by misorientation of the sundial. If the sundial is not correctly oriented, then the shadow falls on the wrong place and gives a false reading of the time. And for those who travelled about and carried a portable dial with them, the gnomon would sometimes be at the wrong angle to the horizontal, or, for the bowl type of sundial, it might not be held exactly level, which would also cause the shadow to fall in the wrong place.

Poor people, who did not have a sundial, would estimate the time by the Sun's position in the sky. Probably the average error in judging the time from the Sun's apparent position is nearly an hour except at sunrise, noon, and sunset, when the error might average 15 minutes.

At night, time was probably read from a water clock. It could, of course, be determined with considerable accuracy by those with astronomical knowledge by observing the constellations and making a calculation based on the culminating constellation and the calendar date. But it is doubtful that this procedure was used in practice. A well-made water clock would drip water at a fairly constant rate, but such a device kept mean time, while what was wanted was seasonal time. An astrologer might know how to convert mean time to seasonal time, but his clients probably would not. I would estimate that the average error of a night time birth would be plus or minus one hour, except at sunset or sunrise, where it might be about 15 minutes.

Second, selecting the correct table depended upon an accurate knowledge of the clime (latitude). We may suppose that the typical astrologer knew the climes of major cities and estimated the climes of others by estimating how far north or south the place was from one of the cities whose clime he knew. Obviously this could easily cause the astrologer to miss the clime by 1 (e.g., 3rd Clime instead of 4th Clime, or vice versa). Hence, he might use the wrong table of rising times. The likelihood of error would be greater for obscure places whose geographical location was uncertain (e.g., "somewhere in central or northern Germany").

Third, the rising times of the arithmetic progression have an average error of several degrees. Here is a table showing the arithmetic rising times for Alexandria and the correct rising times calculated from modern astronomical data. The epoch is July 137 A.D.

	Arith.	*Calc.*	
Aries	21°40′	20°44′	Pisces
Taurus	25°00′	24°03′	Aquarius
Gemini	28°20′	29°48′	Capricorn
Cancer	31°40′	34°39′	Sagittarius
Leo	35°00′	35°46′	Scorpio
Virgo	38°20′	35°00′	Libra

The average error is 1°44′, with the greatest errors in Cancer, Leo, and Virgo (and in the opposite signs, Capricorn, Aquarius, and Pisces. Most of the error arises from the fact that the arithmetic series is only an approximation to accurately calculated spherical arcs, the remainder is due to the fact that the arithmetic series is calculated for about a degree south of Alexandria, while the calculated series uses the actual latitude (31N13) and also an accurate value of the mean obliquity of the ecliptic (23°40'40″ in 137.5 A.D. rather than the 23°51'20″ adopted by Ptolemy. By Paul's time the mean value of the obliquity had decreased to 23°38'52″).

In short, the average error of determining the ASC degree in Alexandria using the arithmetic rising times was perhaps about plus or minus 2°, and the maximum error about 4°. Combining this error with the clock error, we get about plus or minus 10° for a day birth and 17° for a night birth. The average of these errors is 13°30'. This probably means that 45% of the charts erected by the classical astrologers had the wrong rising sign!

6. CALCULATION OF THE MC DEGREE FROM THE ASC DEGREE.

In Chapter 30 Paul explains how to calculate the MC degree from the ASC degree. His method is sound in principle, but defective in details; hence, it only yields an approximate result, but he evidently believed it to be exact, for he calculated the MC down to a fraction of a degree. In modern terms, he calculates the Semi-diurnal arc of the ASC degree, subtracts it from the longitude of the ASC degree, and obtains the longitude of the MC. This is incorrect in two respects: (1) he should subtract the SD arc from the RA of the ASC degree; and (2) he should consider the result to be the RA of the MC rather than its longitude. In a worst case, which is very nearly that of his example, his procedure incurs an error of 2.5 degrees at the ASC end and another 2.5 degrees at the MC end, for a total error of 5 degrees due to his neglect of the necessary conversions from longitude to RA and from RA to longitude.

To this source of error is added the error in the rising times of the signs that results from his use of the arithmetic rising times rather than trigonometrically calculated rising times. This could amount to several degrees. And finally, he takes a simple proportion of the rising time of the ASC sign, which is not quite correct, although that error is small.

All in all, even in low latitudes such as Alexandria, in a worst case the error incurred in Paul's method of calculating the longitude of the MC degree from the longitude of the ASC degree could amount to 10 degrees or more. And to this source of error we would have to add whatever error was incurred in calculating the ASC degree in the first place.

Thus we see that astrologers who followed Paul's method might in a worst case have an error in the calculated MC degree of more than 20 degrees! But fortunately this was a matter of small consequence, for the classical astrologers paid little attention to the MC degree, evidently considering it as more of a curiosity than anything else. Nearly all the ancient references to the "midheaven" refer to the 10th house, not the astronomical MC degree.

Modern astrologers, accustomed to calculating the RAMC first, and from it calculating the ASC, may wonder at the reversed procedure of the classical astrologers. The reason is that in modern times the time of day is reckoned from midnight and noon, while in classical times the time of day was reckoned from sunrise and sunset.

INDEX OF PERSONS

Antiochus of Athens, *astrologer* xviii,16n.1,16n.3,39n.1

Apollinaris, astrologer xi,1

Apollonius of Laodice xi,1

Augustus, Emperor 148, 149n.1

Bethen, *astrologer* xii

Bezza, Giuseppe, *translator* xxii,177

al-Bîrûnî, *science writer* xii

Boer, Emilie, *scholar* xv,xvi,xvii,xviii,40,72,74,82,83,85,89,110,
111,115,143,174

Boll, Franz, *scholar* xi,173

Bonatti, Guido, *astrologer* xii

Bouché-Leclercq, A, *scholar* xin.1,40n.1,146,173

Caesar, Caius Julius, Dictator viii

Caracalla, Emperor viii

Cardan, Jerome, *astrologer* xii,173

Catherine de Médicis, Queen of France vii

Christians viii,149

Cipolla, Jack, *artist* xxi

Constantine the Great, Emperor viii

Cronamon ix,1,2n.3,70n.1,143,144

Cumont, Franz, *scholar* xx,vin.2,52n.2,54n.1,54,n.2,54n.3

Diocletian, Emperor xii,33,34,35,65n.3,98,99,100,148,149,150,
151,152,155

Dorotheus of Sidon, *astrologer* 39n.1,136,173

Egyptians viii,ix,x,xxiii,xxvi,xi,2,7,9,40n.2,73,77,79,85,149

Firmicus Maternus, Julius, *astrologer* xxin.1,119n.1,viii,174

Geminus of Rhodes, *astronomer* 17.n.3,146,147,174

Goold, G. P., *scholar* xii,70n.2,175

Greeks viii,xv,xxi,97

Greenbaum, Dorian Gieseler, *translator* xxii,176

Gundel, Hans Georg, *scholar* 5

Gundel, Wilhelm, *scholar* xi

Heliodorus. *scholar* xv,xin.1,xxi,25n.2,32n.1,40n2,59n.2,61n.2,
65n.3,71n.1,72n.2,73n.2,82n.2,88n.2,89n.2,89n.3,106,119,153,1
55,174

Hephaestio of Thebes, *astrologer* vii,1n.2,16n.3,39n.1,80n.3,
148,174

Hermes Trismegistus, *astrologer* vii,xi,xiii,10,41,78,102,119,
122,127,128

Holden, James Herschel, *translator* 107n.1,174,175,177,178

Housman, A. E., *scholar* 147,175

Huraut, Jean, Sieur de Boistaille, *diplomat* xvii

Hypsicles, *mathematician* 7n.3,157,158,161,175

Ibn Ezra, Abraham, *scholar* xii

Jews viii,150

Manetho, *astrologer* vii

Mirti, Grazia, *astrologer* xix

Nechepso, *astrologer* vii,xi

Neugebauer, Otto, *scholar* xii,25n.2,26n.1,27n.1,38n.1,46n.3,
101n.1,110n.2,111n.1,111n.2,115n.1,143,158,175

Olympiodorus, *astrologer* xin.1,xxi,xxii

Petosiris, *astrologer* vii,xi

Pingree, David, *scholar* xii,38n.1,173,174

Pompey the Great, *statesman* viii

Porphyry, *philosopher* 16n.1,16n.3,25n.2,39n.1,40n.1,84,85n.2, 147,148,177

Ptolemy, Claudius, *science writer* vii,ix,xi,xii,xvii,xviii,12n.1, 16n.1,16n.3,17n.3,24n.2,27,32n.1,32n.2,39n1,41n.1,48n.3,62n.4, 63n.1,65,701n.2,74n.2,77n.3,82n.3,85,90n.4,96n.1,96n.4,101, 114,147,148,153,154,155,163,166,177,178

Rhetorius the Egyptian, *astrologer* vii,16n.1,16n.3,39n.1,52n.2, 86n.2,101n.2,148,178

Riske, Kris Brandt, *editor* xxi

Robbins, F. E., *scholar* xvii

Schato, Andreas, *editor* xv

Schmidt, Robert, *translator* xxii

Scott, Walter, *scholar* 10n.1,174

Stobaeus, Ioannes, *anthologist* 10n.1

Teucer of Babylon, *astrologer* NOT FOUND

Trajan, Marcus Ulpius, Emperor viii

Van Hoesen, H. B., *scholar* xii,46n.3,143

Vettius Valens, *astrologer* vii,1n.2,28n.1,46n.3,85n.4,107n.2, 114n.2,127n.2,136,145,147,149n.1,161,162,163,179

Wright, R. Ramsay, *translator* xii

BIBLIOGRAPHY

Boll, Franz
Sphaera.
Leipzig: B. G. Teubner, 1903.
Hildesheim: Georg Olms, 1967. repr

Bouché-LeClercq, A.
L'Astrologie Grecque.
Paris: Leroux, 1899.
Brussels: Culture et Civilisation, 1963. repr.

Catalogus Codicum Astrologorum Graecorum.
cited herein as CCAG
various editors
Brussels: Various Publishers, 1898-1953. 12 vols.

Cardan, Jerome
Opera Omnia.
Lyons: Huguet & Ravaud, 1663. 10 vols.
New York & London: Johnson Reprint, 1967. 10 vols. repr.

Dorotheus of Sidon
Dorothei Sidoni Carmen astrologicum.
[the Arabic version ed. & trans. by David Pingree,
with Greek citations of the *Pentateuch*, and a
re-edition of some chapters of the *Liber Hermetis*]
Leipzig: B.G. Teubner, 1976.

Firmicus Maternus, Julius
Iulii Firmici Materni Matheseos libri VIII.
ed. W. Kroll, F. Skutsch, and K. Ziegler
Leipzig: B. G. Teubner, 1907-1913. 2 vols.
Leipzig: B. G. Teubner, 1968. 2 vols. repr.

Mathesis.
trans. by James Herschel Holden
Tempe, Az.: A.F.A., Inc., 2011.

Geminus
Géminos: Introduction aux Phénomènes.
ed. & trans. by Germaine Aujac
Paris: Société d'Édition "Les Belles Lettres," 1975.

Heliodorus
Heliodori, ut dicitur, in Paulum
Alexandrinum commentarium.
ed. Emilie Boer
Leipzig: B.G. Teubner, 1962.

Hephaestio of Thebes
Hephaestionis Thebani Apotelesmaticorum libri tres.
ed. by David Pingree
Leipzig: B.G. Teubner, 1973.

Hermetica.
ed. & trans. by Walter Scott
Oxford: Oxford University Press, 1925. 4 vols.
London: Dawsons of Pall Mall, 1968. 4 vols. repr.

Holden, James Herschel
A History of Horoscopic Astrology.
Tempe, Arizona: A.F.A., Inc., 1996. paper xv,359 pp. 21 cm.
Tempe, Arizona: A.F.A., Inc., 2006. paper 2nd ed. rev. xviii,378
pp. 21 cm.

Hypsikles
Die Augangszeiten der Gestirne.
ed. & trans. by V. de Falco & M. Krause
with an introduction by O. Neugebauer
Göttingen: Vandenhoeck & Ruprecht, 1966.

Journal of Research of the
American Federation of Astrologers.
Tempe, Ariz.: A.F.A., Inc., 1982-

Manilius, Marcus
Astronomicon.
ed. & commen. by A. E. Housman
Cambridge: Cambridge Univ. Press, 1937. 5 vols, repr.

Astronomica.
[same book: different title]
ed. & trans. by G. P. Goold
Cambridge, Mass.: Harvard Univ. Press
London: William Heinemann, Ltd., 1977.

Neugebauer, O.
A History of Ancient Mathematical Astronomy.
New York, Heidelberg, Berlin: Springer Verlag, 1975. 3 vols.

The Parisian Epitome of Astrological Works.
ed. in the CCAG 8.3, pp. 91-119
Brussels: Henri Lamertin, 1912.

Paul of Alexandria
Pauli Alexandrini elementa apotelesmatica.
ed. Emilie Boer
Leipzig: B. G. Teubner, 1958.

Paulus Alexandrinus
Introductory Matters.
trans. by Robert Schmidt
Berkeley Springs, W. Va.: Golden Hind Press, 1993.

Paolo d'Alessandria
Lineamenti introduttivi alla scienza
della previsione astronomica.
[Introductory Outlines to the Science
of Astronomical Prediction]
trans. into Italian by Giuseppe Bezza
Milan, 1993.

Late Classical Astrology:
Paulus Alexandrinus & Olympiodorus
with the Scholia from later commentators.
trans. by Dorian Giesler Greenbaum
Reston, Virginia: ARHAT Publications, 2002. comb-binding
177 pp. 29 cm.

Pliny
Natural History.
trans. by H. Rackham, W. H. S. Jones, and D. E. Eichholz
Cambridge, Mass.: Harvard Univ. Press
London: William Heinemann, Ltd., 1949-1970. 10 vols.

Porphyry
Introductio in Tetrabiblum Ptolemaei.
ed. Emilie Boer & Stephen Weinstock
Catalogus Codicum Astrologicorum Graecorum V.4
Brussels: Belgian Royal Academy, 1940.

Porphyry
Introduction to the Tetrabiblos.
trans. from the Greek by James Herschel Holden
Tempe, Arizona: A.F.A., 2009. paper. xviii,74 pp. 21 cm.

Ptolemy
Handbuch der Astronomie.
[a German trans. of the *Syntaxis*]
trans. by K. Manitius
Leipzig: B. G. Teubner, 1962-1963. 2nd ed. 2 vols.

Ptolemy
Ptolemy's Almagest.
trans. and annotated by G.J. Toomer
with a foreword by Owen Gingrich
Princeton, N.J.: Princeton University Press, 1998.

Ptolemy
Tetrabiblos.
ed. & trans. by F. E. Robbins
London: William Heinemann, Ltd.
Cambridge, Mass.: Harvard Univ. Press, 1940.

Rhetorius the Egyptian
Astrological Compendium.
ed. in the CCAG and elsewhere
trans. by James Herschel Holden
Tempe, Arizona: A.F.A., Inc., 2009. paper xx,224 pp. 21 cm.

Sahl ibn Bishr
The Introduction to the Science
of the Judgments of the Stars.
trans. by James Herschel Holden
Tempe, Arizona: A.F.A., Inc., 2008. paper xxii,213 pp. 21 cm.

Theon of Alexandria
Commentaire de Théon d'Alexandrie,
sur le Livre III de l'Almageste de Ptolemée;
Tables Manuelles des Mouvemens des Astres…
trans. into French by the Abbé Nicolas Halma
Paris: A. Bobée, 1822. in three parts

Varahamihira
Brihat Jataka.
ed. & trans. by V. Subrahmanya Sastri
Bangalore: Sadhana Press, 1971. 2nd ed.

Vettius Valens
Vettii Valentis Antiochieni Anthologiarum libri novem.
ed. by David Pingree
Leipzig: B. G. Teubner, 1986.

Printed in the USA
CPSIA information can be obtained
at www.ICGtesting.com
LVHW092324101023
760763LV00004B/72